Woman

Who God Says She Is!

Eddie Lawrence

FBP
FIRST
BREATH
PUBLICATIONS

Killen, Alabama

Title: Woman

Sub-title: Who God Says She Is!

Copyright © 2007

All Rights Reserved by Eddie Lawrence

ISBN-13: 978-0-9790830-1-3

ISBN-10: 0-9790830-1-X

First Breath Publications

P.O. Box 1228

Killen, Alabama 35645

Author Photo by Faith Blessing Photography

Website: www.faithblessing.com

Cover Design Photo by

Cover Design by First Breath Publications

Table of Contents

Dedication

The emerging of a book is like the rising of a river. The river swells and becomes a force because of the convergence of many streams. This book has been birthed out of many streams of influence coming together in my life. I cannot possibly name all these streams, but as with a river, some streams influencing it are greater than others. Besides the Lord, more than anyone else, my wife has influenced my thinking about the power and mystique of a woman. I have witnessed God's hand upon her in such wonderful and marvelous ways. I am indebted to God for allowing me to experience life with her. She is tireless in her pursuit of Him, in her love for me, and in her devotion to our family. For the past twenty-nine years, we have walked out our covenant together. Mikki, you have been rain from heaven to my soul. I look forward to the years ahead.

I also am grateful for my mother. Mom has been such an inspiration to me through the course of my life. She almost gave her life while giving me mine. She has witnessed God's power in remarkable ways. She was my first congregant as I preached to her alone at the age of eight. Thanks, Mom! You have always encouraged and loved me. I appreciate your devotion to the Lord and to me.

Of course, I must say to my four wonderful children: Andrew, Kara Beth, Elliott and Nathan; thanks for sharing Daddy with the computer. I realize you sacrificed in order for me to spend the time necessary to complete this project. I love you!

I never thought I would author a book about the role of women. To do such a thing, I have had to survive the demolition of strongholds, wrongly held beliefs, and male prejudice. I would have viewed myself as the most unlikely candidate for such a project—but here it is ready for your reading. I am so grateful for the journey down the river. So far, it has been quite a ride.

Eddie Lawrence
January, 2007

Foreword

Never before has it been as critical as it is right now for the Church to grasp and embrace the purposes God designed for the female gender from the beginning. The "gender issue" historically has had as its emphasis the relationship between man and woman, husband and wife. The resolution of those issues is vital. But the gender question goes far beyond the context of marriage; it is the foundational issue on which the Church is based. Only when the male gender and the female gender are walking side by side in the fullness of their calling will the Church be seen in wholeness and the strength God intended for it to impact the earth. God is releasing revelation concerning His plan and purpose for the female gender in this hour, and Eddie Lawrence has heard from the Lord and through this book is imparting truth that is needed in the body of Christ.

Jane Hansen, President/CEO
Aglow International

Introduction

No pessimist ever discovered the secret of the stars or sailed an uncharted land, or opened a new doorway for the human spirit. –
Helen Keller

~

What does the future hold for woman? Will she step into realms of freedom that her predecessors never experienced? I believe the horizons of tomorrow are bright for today's distant daughters of Eve. I believe this is the hour when God Almighty is stepping with power into human history and restoring the powerful voices of women in order to see His good pleasure fulfilled. Wrong mindsets, errant theology, and prejudice toward women are all in the path that God is clearing. This will result in women being fully restored to God's original intended place. It is the time when He is liberating Christian women for the frontlines of ministry to take their places at the sides of men.

I recently read a statement in the 2004 issue paper released by the Lausanne Issue Group 24 concerning the empowering of men and women for ministry. The statement read, *"More than half of the body of Christ are women who are the most undervalued and underutilized resource of the church."*[1] It is a staggering and sobering thought to realize that the majority of believers (women) on the earth today

11

are undervalued and held back by the minority of believers (men). Could it be that we have been praying for the Lord to send forth workers, but we have refused to receive them? Has our gender bias kept us from seeing the fulfillment of the Great Commission? Is a woman's voice so untrustworthy that she should remain silent though we as believers are all mandated to share the good news? Is the blood of Jesus powerful enough to remove the stain of Eve's sin and break through all the male bias and prejudice that has been used by the enemy of women throughout the centuries? Is it possible for women to be restored to the place God originally designed for her? These are questions for which we must give account and for which *we will* give account.

As much as anything else, men filled with religious zeal have held women back from their God ordained destinies. Yet, Jesus Christ, the perfect man, did more to restore value and respect to women than any person who has ever lived. Somewhere in the mix, religion and the actions and teachings of Jesus have parted company when it comes to the women issue. For the most part, religious mankind has built an image of woman that is not the true reflection of who she is. In the first mention of woman in Scripture, God explicitly states that He made her in His image. The truth is- -*woman was God's idea.* She was created to live in authority and dominion. She was not created to be ruled over and dominated. She stood at the side of the first man as they both enjoyed being God's under regents reigning in the earth.

In the moments after the first woman's first failure, the voice of God began decreeing that she would be a weapon in His hand to defeat Satan. He further announced that man would be filled with a desire to rule over her. This conflict between what God *said* and what man *says* still exists when it comes to women. Today, she is seen through a lens still fogged over by Eden's failure. Through this book, we will look through the eyes of Scripture in an attempt to clear up man's foggy notion of *who* woman is. Who does God say a woman is? This is the question to be resolved.

The last thing God created was the first thing Satan attacked.

Woman was the ingenious creation of God to join with man to complete His plans for the world that He had created. He had started with nothing and on each proceeding day He created something more extraordinary than the day before. The last creation of God in Eden's paradise was a woman. She was the last thing God's creative hand touched. Think of it, God's final touch among Eden's wonders was a woman. The last thing God created was the first thing Satan attacked.

She was Adam's wife and Daddy God's girl all in one. She was beautiful and perfect in every way--a 10! She was intelligent, articulate, and bubbling over with the joy of life. The first touch upon her life had been the hand of God. Her first breath had been breathed in the very presence of God. She was awesome! The second being to ever touch her was her husband, Adam. It was pure. It was perfect. Fireworks! I believe God applauded and the angels flapped their wings.

She was created to complete what a man could not do. This fact alone tells us God created her to do things a man could not. The truth is that man is incomplete without her, and she is incomplete without him. Man and woman were originally created in a mutual dependency. What God created as one team has been turned into two teams fighting against each other. Make no mistake about it, *woman was God's idea*. The first man, Adam, agreed with God that she was a great idea. He looked at her and declared, "She's like me!" Adam had already looked among all the other creatures on Earth for a suitable companion and found none. At the first, God allowed him to experience life without a woman so that when she came, he would recognize her value above all other created beings—*and he did*!

If woman was given as a gift from God to man to help complete God's purposes in the earth, then it makes sense to realize the enemy would want to silence her voice. Her voice is needed for man to be complete. Just as Christ carries out His purposes in the earth in partnership with His praying, preaching, and prophesying bride, there is a sense in which man also needs the complimentary voice of woman to complete His work in the earth. Men and women need each other to experience God's complete purposes in the earth. The enemy wants us to compete with each other. God wants us to compliment each other. Before sin ever entered the human race, God decreed that it was not good for man to be alone. Then He made a woman and man was not alone.

Through these pages, we will travel together to discover the precious truth about women. The core of this book is summed up in the questions, "What does God say about women? and "Why are women here?" The answers to these questions are fundamental to a person's basic belief system. If

> **The enemy wants us to compete with each other. God wants us to compliment each other.**

how we behave paints a picture of what we truly believe, then many people today, men and women, truly believe that women are listed in category B on God's list of favorites. It is not true that men were made for the penthouse and women for the basement. There are questions that need to be asked and their answers sought.

- What does God really say about who a woman is?
- What did God have in mind when He created Eve—the first woman?

- Was her fairy tale book beginning just a tease to excite her until she flunked the first test?
- Was it all just a good idea gone bad?
- Was it a utopia relegated to history that is never to be repeated? Or, could it be that God will ultimately have what He originally intended?
- Could it be that what God had in mind was far greater than any of us have imagined? Could it be that His original plan is still in vogue?
- Could it be that He is beginning to bring woman back into her originally intended place of honor and distinction beside the man?
- Could it be that there is much more to a woman than she knows?

In the wonderful beginning of humankind recorded in Genesis, what God had in mind for a woman and what man had in mind for a woman was based on the same fabulous idea. They both deeply loved the image, idea and inspiration that were all part of the first woman. She was perfect in every way. When she spoke, Adam listened. He enjoyed being with her. He was hers—and--she was his. That is—*they were one.* They were inseparable and in love. It is time for the sons of Adam to wake up and see what our great- granddad Adam saw. It is time for us to be filled anew and afresh with the awe of what God did when He made a woman. It is time for the daughters of Eve to receive the love, honor, and respect that the first man gave the first woman. Women around the world are waiting to hear their men give them the love, honor, and respect that were part of the first couple's relationship.

Some argue today that the Church is under the influence of too much feminization. Others argue that the Church is too masculine in its makeup. The aim of this work is to understand God's original intentions for both men and women. The clearer we see what God desires to do in regard to the gender issue, the more confidently we can align our will with His.

It is a rather strange thing, I suppose, for me a man to be writing a book about women. I am the first to admit that I am at a loss to comprehend the way the mind of a woman operates. I also suspect that the majority of the readers who venture into the pages of this book will be feminine in their bearings. Why am I writing about a subject about which I admit a great degree of ignorance? Well, it's not because I have ink in my cartridge, and I have nothing else to write about. It is not an attempt to voice all men's frustrations about their inability to understand women. I have discovered some truths in my study of God's Word that will be absolutely exhilarating and liberating to all who read it.
What can you expect to encounter as you journey through this container in your hands called a book? You will find that its pages will reveal to you that Father God had your future on His heart as He pronounced the curse upon the

serpent. You will engage God in a new way as you realize that He personally prophesied over the first woman to give hope to every woman (Genesis 3:15). You will learn about the power of the decrees of God in bringing your wayward children back home to the Lord. You will discover that woman was destined to be a warrior. The

> **The weaker vessel is truly a powerful warring vessel**.

weaker vessel is truly a powerful warring vessel. In a word, you will confront a "reversal" in some of the ways you have formerly thought about women. I do not say this boastfully, but biblically. I believe that when a woman reads what I will share in this book, her spirit will rise up in boldness, confidence, and authority as never before—not to put men in their place, but to truly take her place as a woman whom God decreed would be a weapon in His hand to topple Satan's empire!

Chapter One
Creating Controversy

The history of the world is but the biography of great men.
Philosopher Thomas Carlyle, 1795-1881

~

There is no denying that women on the planet feel that they are living in a man's world—but is it a man's world?

Whose world is it?
Is it man's?
Is it woman's?
Is it man and woman's?
Is it God's?

The world is God's by virtue of His creative activity, but to whom did He give governance over the Earth? The simple answer from Scripture is that man and woman were both given dominion. Dominion was a *both/and* thing, not an *either/or* thing. Dominion was a God-granted authority given to them together.

Genesis 1: 27 So God created man in His own image; in the image of God He created him; male and female He created them. 28 Then God blessed them, and God said to them, "Be fruitful and multiply; fill the earth and subdue

it; have dominion over the fish of the sea, over the birds of the air, and over every living thing that moves on the earth."

Why is there such upheaval and chaos between the sexes? The simple answer is sin. We'll save the longer version of the answer for a later chapter. For now, suffice it to say, things changed when sin occurred and God's original intentions for the relationship between men and women were not realized. The next question is—*"Will they be realized?"* If so, *"How will it happen?"* and *"What will it look like?"*

We are now in a season where God is restoring women to His originally intended place for her. We should expect to see women gaining the respect of equality from more and more men. The war is not over women being given dominion over men—it is over women standing side by side with men. Both men and women have their respective God-given roles, but neither was

> **The war is not over women being given dominion over men—it is over women standing side by side with men.**

ever intended to exercise dominion over the other. Is there a place for a woman to speak directively into the life of a man? Did Eve's blunder forever seal men's ears to the voice of women? Has God called women into collective silence when it comes to sharing wisdom with men?

Some people think that because Paul wrote that a woman is not to teach a man, that God would *never* use a woman to give spiritual direction to a man. Yet, as Jesus stood before Pontius Pilate, word was sent to him by his wife about a dream she had.

Matt 27:19 While he was sitting on the judgment seat, his wife sent to him, saying, "Have nothing to do with that just Man, for I have suffered many things today in a dream because of Him."

Where did her dream originate? Was it Satan trying to stop the crucifixion? That doesn't square with Scripture. Was she a psychic? Doesn't seem like the forces behind the occult would have taken a stand for Jesus, since He regularly sent demons packing, does it? She also declared Jesus a just man—innocent! It's interesting that she doesn't ask Pilate to consider what she is saying; she simply tells him straight out, *"Have nothing to do with that just man..."* Her statement was more of an order than a request. It sounds like she received revelation from God about the matter, doesn't it?

The truth is God chose to invade the dreams of Pilate's wife. She had a revelatory experience where she saw and experienced things about Jesus. She became aware that her husband was becoming a part of something sinister and unjust, so she warned him. He did not listen to her, but maybe this is what caused him to wash his hands and try to distance himself from the matter. The truth is God chose to speak to Pilate through his wife—a woman. He could have troubled Pilate's sleep, but He did not. He chose a woman. When the innocent Son of God stood before the reigning civil authority of His day, the voice God chose to speak for His innocent Son was the voice of a woman. As a matter of fact, it seems it was the only voice that came before Pilate in Jesus' defense. I believe the message that Pilate received from his wife was a message from God. The point—God has, does, and will speak to men through women. He worked through Deborah, Esther, Ruth, and many other anointed women in the Scriptures. Why would someone think it out of order for God to continue to speak through women today?

This book is written to help open the minds of men and women to this subject. Once minds begin to open to the truth, then everything else that needs to open will begin to open. I believe truth frees us from wrong mindsets. I am aware that there are passages in the New Testament that seem to suggest that women are not to have a part in the teaching or leadership ministry of the entire church. I encourage those desiring to study those passages in detail to read the excellent book, *Why Not Women: A Fresh Look at Scripture on Women in Missions, Ministry, and Leadership.*[2] Loren Cunningham and David Joel Hamilton do an excellent job of looking at the hermeneutics, context, and biblical language in order to rightly divide such passages in light of other very clear passages that demonstrate God's use of women in ministry.

On a practical level, think through the following questions with your own life and the lives of those closest to you in mind:

- How many of you men came to the Lord after your wife began faithfully serving Him?
- How many of you really got serious about Jesus after she did?
- How many of you were taught to pray by your mother or by a woman?
- How many of you had mothers that carried you to church?
- How many of you had a grandmother that loved the Lord?
- How many of you had a woman Sunday School teacher that really influenced you?
- Of the people that have most influenced your life spiritually, how many of them were women?

Most of us have been significantly influenced by women as our spirituality developed and afterwards as well. Thank God for godly mothers! It is interesting to realize that one of the major influences of a person's life during their formative years is their mother. In addition to many other areas, this is part of God's special and creative design for women. The role of women has influence inside and outside the home. Inside and outside the church. Inside and outside the marriage. She is not to be muted into silence. She is to use her gifts, talents, and her voice to the glory of God. Let everything that has breath, praise the Lord—including women!

I am aware that this book will create controversy. I am grateful for the wonderful experiences that I have enjoyed each place I have pastored, and I have very fond and grateful memories of my beloved seminary. They continue to do an awesome job of preparing ministers to enter the mission field and church field. However, I have experienced several areas of change concerning my beliefs since my seminary days. The bulk of what I received I still hold dearly. I have great respect and admiration for my professors, fellow students and pastors. I still consider myself very conservative theologically. I believe the Book! I also believe that the Holy Spirit will guide us into all truth. Nevertheless, I have come to realize that we often wear lenses that distort what we see as we read the Bible. We need to pray, *"Lord give us eyes to see and ears to understand."* Jesus informed the religious leaders of His day that they were not really seeing what the Word said.

John 5:39 You search the Scriptures, for in them you think you have eternal life; and these are they which testify of Me. 40 But you are not willing to come to Me that you may have life. 41 I do not receive honor from men.

We must not interpret the Bible by the buddy system. Too often, we simply parrot what we have been taught instead of studying the Scripture for ourselves. Thank God for good teachers, good books, and seasoned theologians. However, we must not allow the fear of the disapproval of

> **The new and unfamiliar is often feared by all of us who have chosen to live in the comfort zone.**

man to keep us from embracing truth. Truth transforms us as we obey it. Martin Luther was branded a heretic by his "buddies." The Wesley brothers drew the ire of their compatriots. Finney was criticized by pastors for his unorthodox beliefs and practices. I am not placing myself alongside these giants of the faith; I am just saying forerunners have to wade through the briars and thickets clearing a path that makes it easier for those who follow. The new and unfamiliar is often feared by all of us who have chosen to live in the comfort zone. The Lord has a way of confronting us with the truth we say we believe in order for it be become settled in our hearts. In this season, He is raising up people who will trumpet the truth concerning the restoration of the voice of women. The following story illustrates how this can happen.

Recently, as I was completing this book, my family and I attended the mid-year graduation ceremony at the University of North Alabama to celebrate with our nephew who was receiving his undergraduate degree. The place was packed, and we ended up sitting in the nose bleed section. As I scanned through the program, I noticed the special speaker who had been invited to deliver the commencement address was the Senior Pastor of Fern Creek Baptist Church in Louisville, Kentucky. The thing that stood out was that this Senior Pastor was a woman-- Rev. Linda Barnes Popham. Linda grew up in our area and had graduated from the University of North Alabama. I immediately started running material through the ole thought mill in my head:

This was a bold step on the part of the school's president.
What will this crowd think about a woman pastor as the commencement speaker?
Will they heckle her?
Will they applaud her?
We are in the center of the Bible Belt, who would have figured this?
Is she an extreme theological liberal?

I then began to process what was going on in my own heart and mind:

How strange this has happened in our city while I am writing a book about the restoration of a woman's voice.
Why do I feel uncomfortable seeing this in the program?
Why am I assuming she may be extremely liberal?
I think I remember her name from somewhere.

She was the center of controversy in the SBC just after I graduated seminary.
I remember now! I remember how I felt back in the early nineties when her church was voting on her to become their Senior Pastor.

In that moment there was a collision of who I had been and who I had become. I had to deal with the resurgence of feelings that reminded me of my critical tongue and the judgment that had ruled in my heart.

I sat through the first part of the service wondering what would happen once Rev. Popham took the podium. The time came for President William Cale to introduce her. As she stepped to the podium, there was a gracious but meager applause. I thought, *This is going to be interesting*. She began speaking. I quickly accessed, *She is confident, articulate, and very personable.* Would I have made the same observations about a man? My own newly formed convictions were being challenged and I was grateful. It is important that we come to the place where convictions become settled because they have been tested. People could sense the tension in the room. The crowd knew the vast majority of Alabama Bible Belt believers in the auditorium were being put to the test. Even those who were not believers were aware of the cultural stretching occurring in the room. No one knew it more than Linda Barnes Popham. I am sure questions were whirling in people's mind.

She was within the borders of her own hometown, what would her countryman do?
What would she do?
Would she address the issue?
Would she graciously ignore it?
Would she tackle it head on?
How would she approach our mindsets if she did take it on?

As she proceeded, she did take it on, head on. She shared the struggles of the trials and mistreatment her path had led her through. She encouraged the graduating students not to be deterred by the obstacles that would try to block their paths. At one point, you could hear mumbling among the people beginning to arise, but it quickly subsided. She shared that she was one of around 40 women who served as Senior Pastors out of more than 40,000 churches in the Southern Baptist Convention. She informed us that there were two women Senior Pastors in Baptist churches in the state of Alabama—the same as Kentucky, the state in which she pastored. She shared some of the conversations she had experienced among her peers like the time she called one of the denominational offices and was told she did not exist. Interestingly, she stated that the greatest obstacle she had to face was other women—not men. The statement surprised me. She also gave a bold and courageous challenge to the whole building to stop holding back the voices that wanted to spread the Good News.

She's a feisty fighter, I found myself thinking. The best was yet to come. She then gave a very bold witness for Jesus Christ. Unashamedly and uncompromisingly, she shared that He was the passion of her life and that her main desire was to see people come to a saving knowledge of Jesus Christ. I thought, *Wow! She is bold and courageous!* In the middle of a secular institution on their big night, she preached Christ. Would a man have done so? Would most men have used the opportunity to glorify Christ or would we have thrown a few hints hoping people would fill in the blanks? She left no blanks to fill in. Regardless of what people thought about her right to be a Senior Pastor, they could not deny she had a passion for people to know Jesus Christ. I do not know Linda Barnes Popham. I do not know all that she believes, and I know little of her personal history. This is not my disclaimer, just the truth. However, I do believe she loves Jesus and He was pleased with the way she shared Him with an audience that was doubtless filled with people who needed to know of His great love. When she finished, there was a wonderful applause from the people. I was proud of her and I was proud of the way an Alabama Bible Belt audience graciously honored her.

I am raising questions that will cause us to seek answers. I am challenging all of us to rethink what we think about the voices of women in the body of Christ. The term "woman preacher" is a hot button in many camps and fighting words for more than a few.

- Should a woman preach the gospel where men are present?
- Can a woman biblically teach men?
- Are women to remain silent in public worship?
- Is she limited to just sharing a testimony or teaching women and children?

What does the Word of God teach us that Jesus thought about the subject? *Find out what Jesus said and stick with it!* This is good advice for any of us. I remember as a Baptist pastor on several occasions when a woman spoke in our services that I was always careful to say that "Sister _____ is going to share a testimony with us tonight." This was the safety net. Usually, she would preach, and we would talk about the wonderful way she shared her testimony or gave her report. These word games are still played.

Luther's battle in what we now call the Protestant Reformation yielded the cry of *Sola Scriptura.* He started a revolution insisting that the Bible alone should serve as the basis of authority in the Church. At the core of what Luther and his followers heralded was the doctrine of the priesthood of all believers. In other words, all believers had access to God directly. There was no need to go through any other human mediator because Christ was the mediator of the New Testament and every believer was represented by

Him. The reformation birthed many changes. The new movement began putting the Scriptures in the hands of the common man and woman. Men who were priests began to marry. Women who were nuns began to marry. Prayers were offered in the language of the people instead of Latin. Believing that all believers had direct access to God without any human mediation became a cultural bulldozer clearing a new path by which people worshipped God. Yet today many people who feel it is alright for a woman to talk directly with God still wince at the notion that she can talk directly to mere men. She can share her heart with God, but in many places she cannot share her heart with an audience where men are present. God's door is open; but, for the most part, man's door remains closed.

> **The Barna Research Group indicates "that women shoulder most of the responsibility for the health and vitality of the Christian faith in the country."**

What is the value of women in the life of the church today? The Barna Research Group indicates "that women shoulder most of the responsibility for the health and vitality of the Christian faith in the country."[3] Barna also states that among born again believers in America that there are 11 to 13 million more women than men. However in leadership in the churches, over 90% of Senior Pastors are men.[4] I do not believe that the core of the war is about getting women into positions of Senior Pastor; it is about men valuing the voice of women—period! Side by side they are to stand receiving from one another in the fullness of Christ. Until men are ready to hear what women say, the words of women will not be readily received or redemptively heard.

My wife and I talked about the aforementioned graduation experience on the way home that night as well as the next morning. We both agreed that the timing of the writing of this book and the graduation experience was uncanny and that God was saying something to us through it. We realized that this book would be controversial. More than likely, it would bring both trouble and blessing to us. The conclusion was, **"Will of God, be done!"**

Chapter Two
The Helper

Because I am a woman, I must make unusual efforts to succeed. If I fail, no one will say, "She doesn't have what it takes." They will say, "Women don't have what it takes." –Clare Boothe Luce

~

Women who do not understand what the Bible really says about them can become bitter and feel like unwanted, underprivileged children. They can also become disenchanted with the whole male species and write them off. Case in point is Gloria Steinem, who is a modern day activist and founder of the Women's Political Caucus, who articulated her estimate of men when she said, *"A woman without a man is like a fish without a bicycle."*[5] While humorous, it is sad when one half of the whole human race can be regarded as unneeded by the other half. I suppose there is plenty of evidence to convict both genders of this kind of thinking. The truth is that we need each other. Men need women and women need men to make things on the planet travel in God's intended direction. The Bible teaches us that woman was created to help man.

Some women react negatively to the description "helpmate" or "helper" as applied to their purpose on the planet. Some men use it in a way that makes the woman feel inferior in her position. Did God get it wrong when He declared the woman to be Adam's helper?

Gen 2:18 And the LORD God said, "It is not good that man should be alone; I will make him a helper comparable to him."

This verse reveals to us what was on God's heart as He proceeded to create Adam's helper. Remember, this declaration of God was before sin entered the human race. In other words, whatever a helper was to be, it was good and very good. There was no suggestion of second-place attached to it. Before the Fall of humankind, the notion of competition and unhealthy comparison did not exist. Only the experiential knowledge of evil would cause Adam and Eve to diminish each other in any way. Since God stated that Eve was to be a suitable helper, then the understanding of the term "helper" is vital to women understanding their God ordained destinies. Let's press the fast-forward button for a moment and move from the book of Genesis to the book of John.

Before the Fall of humankind, the notion of competition and unhealthy comparison did not exist.

In the New Testament, we are told that the Holy Spirit would come and serve as our "Helper". The following verses from John's Gospel were given to the disciples by

Jesus just hours before He was crucified. They teach us that the Holy Spirit has been given to us to help us in some vital and exciting ways. Because of the help of the Holy Spirit, we are able to know and accomplish things we could not otherwise know and accomplish. Notice the ways the Holy Spirit helps the believer.

John 14:16 And I will pray the Father, and He will give you another Helper, that He may abide with you forever — 17 the Spirit of truth, whom the world cannot receive, because it neither sees Him nor knows Him; but you know Him, for He dwells with you and will be in you. 18 I will not leave you orphans; I will come to you.

John 14: 26 But the Helper , the Holy Spirit, whom the Father will send in My name, He will teach you all things, and bring to your remembrance all things that I said to you.

John 15:26 But when the Helper comes, whom I shall send to you from the Father, the Spirit of truth who proceeds from the Father, He will testify of Me.

John 16:7 Nevertheless I tell you the truth. It is to your advantage that I go away; for if I do not go away, the Helper will not come to you; but if I depart, I will send Him to you.

Do you think it takes away from the Holy Spirit to refer to Him as a helper? Would Jesus designate a term to describe the Holy Spirit that would cause us to think less of Him? No! Jesus would never do that. Helper is a term that denotes value and purpose.

The writer of Hebrews teaches us that Jesus is also our helper. Does this lessen who Jesus is to refer to Him as our helper?

Hebrews 13:5 Let your conduct be without covetousness; be content with such things as you have. For He Himself has said, "I will never leave you nor forsake you."   6 So we may boldly say:

"The LORD is my helper ;
I will not fear.
What can man do to me?"

In the Old Testament, God Himself is often referred to as our Helper. Read the following verses and ask yourself, "Does it take away from God or lessen His standing to think of Him in terms of being our Helper?"

Gen 49:25 By the God of your father who will help you, And by the Almighty who will bless you

Ps 10:14…You are the helper of the fatherless.

Ps 30:10 Hear, O LORD, and have mercy on me;
LORD, be my helper !"

Ps 54:4 Behold, God is my helper ;
The Lord is with those who uphold my life.
5 He will repay my enemies for their evil.
Cut them off in Your truth.

Ps 20:2 May He send you help from the sanctuary,
And strengthen you out of Zion;

Ps 121:1 I will lift up my eyes to the hills —
From whence comes my help?
2 My help comes from the LORD,
Who made heaven and earth.

It is clear from the preceding Scriptures that being a helper is a positive and powerful thing. God as our Helper rescues us, enables us, provides for us, leads us, and does things for us that we cannot do for ourselves.

Instead of viewing the term "helper" as a slam, we should view it as a lofty expression. When someone helps us, it means that they are supplying their strength to us in order to compensate for our weakness. Though perfect, there were some things Adam could not do without Eve. She had to help him in order for God's purposes to be fulfilled in his life. Conversely, Adam was necessary to Eve in order for her to fulfill God's plans for her life. They needed each other, but not in a deficient or sinful way. They needed each other to be able to complete their divine assignments.

> In biblical terms, the helper is the greater one because the helper furnishes what the one in need does not have.

Adam was first in order of creation, but that does not mean he was first in order of importance or status. The truth is that the two of them became one before God. The man and the woman together became the full expression of humankind. There was no competition or unhealthy comparison. There was mutual satisfaction, joy, and fullness of life and purpose. In our culture, helper implies a novice, one who does not know as much as the one that is being assisted. In biblical terms, the helper is the greater one because the helper furnishes what the one in need does not have. In this sense, woman provided for the man that which he did not have.

Chapter Three
The Decree

For most of history, Anonymous was a woman.
Virginia Woolf (1882 - 1941)

~

What were the first things God said about women? What were the first things He said about women after sin entered the human race? Since God had the first say and He will have the last say about women, what He says should affect what we say about women. What God says on a subject is important. When He speaks in regard to an issue, we would be wise to listen.

Christians believe that Jesus is the Christ, the Son of the Living God, born of a virgin, who lived a sinless life and died a sacrificial death to redeem mankind. We believe that God raised Jesus from the dead, He appeared to many witnesses over a forty day period, and ascended to be seated at the right hand of God the Father. Most Christians believe that Jesus will return to the earth some day to make all things new. Until His return, we are to be empowered by His Holy Spirit to be witnesses of the Gospel—the message that He died, was buried, and raised from the dead on the third day to save us from our sins. These confessions of faith are very important to us. It should go without saying that we believe they are important to the Lord as well. Therefore, it should cause us to think a little bit, when we realize that Jesus gave to a team of two women the responsibility to announce for the very first time the world's most important message.

The first thing lost to sin was the first thing restored by the resurrected Jesus—the power of a woman's voice.

This gives us great insight into the heart of Jesus toward women. He knew women had suffered a long time since the days of Eve. He knew Father had said He would use a woman to bring forth a Seed that would change things. The first thing lost to sin was the first thing restored by the resurrected Jesus—the power of a woman's voice. The Gospel writers inform us that the first witnesses of the resurrection were women. As a matter of fact, Matthew records that the women were told by an angel to deliver the news to the men. This was not the cultural norm of the day! The first men to ever hear the gospel preached in its fullness, heard it from the lips of a woman. This was very significant. The Angel said:

Matt 28:7 And go quickly and tell His disciples that He is risen from the dead, and indeed He is going before you into Galilee; there you will see Him. Behold, I have told you."

The next verse shows us another thing that happened that underscored that Jesus wanted a woman to be the first herald of the Gospel. As they went, Jesus appeared to them, and He personally told them to go and announce what had happened.

Matt 28:9 And as they went to tell His disciples, behold, Jesus met them, saying, "Rejoice!" So they came and held Him by the feet and worshiped Him. 10 Then Jesus said to them, "Do not be afraid. Go and tell My brethren to go to Galilee, and there they will see Me."

What Jesus did as His very first act after He conquered death should be very significant to us. He appeared to women and told them to share the good news with the disciples. No sweeter message had ever been delivered by a human being. The first woman's voice was used by the serpent to spread a lie, so Jesus used a woman's voice first to spread the truth. A daughter of Eve was the first to announce the news that confirmed God's promise to the first woman had been kept.

> **A daughter of Eve was the first to announce the news that confirmed God's promise to the first woman had been kept.**

Whatever you read in the rest of the New Testament, you should not discard this fact. When you read that Paul says that women are to keep quiet and not teach men, it should be read keeping in mind what Jesus did on the first resurrection morning (1 Cor. 14:34, 1 Ti, 2:12). Are they contradictory? No! Obviously, Paul would not make a statement he intended to become a blanket statement overruling the clear practice of Jesus Himself. So then, we should

> **The first men to ever hear the gospel preached in its fullness, heard it from the lips of a woman. This was very significant.**

expect that there was some specific temporary problem that Paul was addressing or we are not interpreting the passage correctly. Historical and grammatical research both indicate the passage has been generally misunderstood. The epistles will always rest upon and never contradict the revelation of Jesus Himself. At His ascension, Jesus told His disciples to tarry in Jerusalem and wait for the enduement of power of the Holy Spirit. It was Peter and eleven other men who were at the forefront on the day of Pentecost. This would be expected in such a male dominated culture. Luke, however, records for us that the period of waiting and praying included men and women together.

Acts 1:14 These all continued with one accord in prayer and supplication, with the women and Mary the mother of Jesus, and with His brothers.

If Peter and the disciples felt that women were not to pray with men or meet with men, then why are the women there? The passage clearly states that **they "all" continued with "one accord" in prayer....**(emphasis added) Was it wrong for them to be obeying Jesus' orders to tarry in Jerusalem with the men? If the men felt like the Lord would have been displeased with the inclusion of women, then why are the women there? Is it safe to say that they were there because they all knew that is the way the Lord wanted it? Was the great commission for the whole church or just the male minority? Acts 1:15 goes on to tell us the total number of disciples gathered was about 120. While there, they chose a replacement for Judas. That they look for a man and not a woman is clear. Yet when the Spirit fell on Pentecost, the announcement came that the gift of the Father that empowers witnesses is for all. Things shifted on the day of Pentecost. What Jesus commanded the women to do on the first day of the resurrection was verified by supernatural phenomenon and a prophetic promise on the day of Pentecost. We will look at this more closely in Chapter Nine, *The Restoration of All Things.* So, I wanted you to see that Jesus chose women to announce the good news that death had been defeated—the curse had been broken. Now let's look at what Father God decreed when the first woman fell into sin. This passage also gives us great insight into the heart of God toward women. The following passage was spoken to the serpent by God Himself just after Eve had been deceived. It also helps us understand Jesus' role in the restoring the voice of woman.

**Genesis 3:15 And I will put enmity
Between you and the woman,
And between your seed and her Seed;
He shall bruise your head,
And you shall bruise His heel."**

In Eve's greatest moment of failure, weakness, and guilt, God released a decree that shaped the future of all women. Within the hearing of the fallen woman, while speaking to the serpent, a great word of hope was released to her. God decreed her success. A decree is a judicial pronouncement. In the case of Genesis 3:15, that decree sealed Satan's defeat.

> In Eve's greatest moment of failure, weakness, and guilt, God released a decree that shaped the future of all women.

- God spoke.
- Heaven issued a decree.
- All God's power stood behind what God spoke.
- The decree sealed Satan's doom.
- The decree insured Woman's success.
- The decree paved the way for redemption.
- The decree was God's verdict of ultimate victory.

- The decree drew a line and placed the woman on God's side of redemptive history.
- The decree demonstrated what God thinks of women.
- The decree revealed the destiny of mankind.
- The decree announced the first coming of Jesus Christ.
- The decree announced Christ's death and His victory over it.
- The decree announced the woman's comeback.
- The decree announced God's intention to reverse the curse and restore fallen humanity.

Satan started hearing about what Jesus was going to do to him as soon as Adam and Eve sinned. This powerful decree shows us the nature of Father God's heart and His desire for fallen woman. With her neck, as it were, under the serpent's foot, God said I'm going to use the woman to turn this thing around. It is the nature of Father God to respond to His children's weakness with His power. When He shows up in the dark moments of our lives, He sheds light to enable us to see again. The serpent came to the garden to feed on human flesh and he left eating dust. Death was released on humanity but a future Seed was prophesied to overcome it. The nature of the prophetic is that it gives hope. Adam and Eve's hanging heads were lifted by the powerful decree God released to the serpent. Though they faced drastic and deadly changes in their lives, they were given a word to hold in their hearts.

We can all learn from the ways that God does business. In the passage of Scripture we refer to as the pronouncement of the curse, we actually find the pronouncement of the cure. We will either be possessed by a curse mentality or a cure mentality. When it comes to the world's mindset toward women, it is the curse mentality that has taken the lead. Thank God that this is changing in our day.

What happened after God came into the garden to address the fallen man and woman is astounding and forms a large part of the foundation of this book. It involves a prophetic decree made by God Himself. I believe it is the first prophetic word recorded in Scripture. It came from God's mouth, and it involved the woman, her kids, Jesus, and the serpent. God did not engage in a verbal volley with Adam or Eve. He did not argue with them. Why should God argue, He has nothing to prove. God asks the questions. The man points to the woman and the woman points to the snake. Once Eve directed God's question toward the serpent, He began to address the serpent. He stepped up to the bully! What He said to the serpent released the power of righteousness full-scale against the power of deception and evil. His judicial decree over the serpent was also a decree of liberation over the woman. Allow me to very loosely paraphrase the gist of what God said:

"You will regret deceiving this woman. From now on women will be your enemy. They will have children who will also be your

enemies. Ultimately, a child will be born and you will bruise His heel, but He will crush your head."

Wow! You get the sense that God is ticked off at the snake for messing with His little girl. He stepped in between her and the bully and let the bully have it. He knew He would deal with her disobedience later, but He informs the serpent with a "You've done the wrong thing now! Before it's over, you will regret that this day ever happened. Mr. Snake— You are going to pay!" The Woman—Daddy's daughter-- who had failed is now decreed by God Himself to be His means of turning it all around. He will work through women to reverse the curse. She will be His means of delivering the deliverer. With the sentence of death hanging over her head and the future of all humankind, God prophesies her comeback! What hope this must have infused into Eve's heart as she overheard her Father God giving the serpent a proverbial ear full. Don't you know this sent a "Daddy is going to take care of it!" through her trembling soul. I contend that there is power in this verse for women today. Note what the writer of the well-respected Biblical Illustrator had to say:

"I will put enmity between thee and the woman. Here it is worth while to notice that the Hebrew tense admits of a present as well as a future interpretation. So it is not only, "I will put enmity"; but, "I am putting and will put enmity between thee and the woman." The work is

begun. The unholy alliance, into which Eve had been beguiled by the Evil One, is already broken. She is already a changed woman. She is no longer on the serpent's side. She is on the Lord's side. There is enmity between her and the serpent.[6]"

This is powerful to consider. God decreed the woman on His side, and He on her side. It was a statement that carried authority to strengthen Eve in that historical moment and to provide hope and strength for women to come. Now in Christ, the promise lives on in the present power of the Holy Spirit imparting to women what they need to be crushers of the serpent's head. Through the resident indwelling power of the risen Christ, women today can take their heels and in Jesus' name crush the enemy. As such, women are daring warriors who are Satan's nightmare. At the moment Eve became an enemy of Satan, the Word was in place for every woman to become an enemy of Satan.

Have you ever thought about the fact that it is an honor to be referred to as Satan's enemy? It is true that you can tell a lot about a person by those who oppose them. There is an old saying that goes, "If you never run into the Devil, you might be running with him!" There's a lot of truth in this old saying. Throughout history the enemy has been running into warrior women clinging to the promises of God.

Now let's tie together the scenes of two gardens. One is the Garden of Eden. The other is the garden where the tomb of Jesus was located. **This is a beautiful picture I had never seen before.** Please read again the passage used earlier in this chapter that describes Jesus appearing to the women as they left the tomb.

Matt 28:9 And as they went to tell His disciples, behold, Jesus met them, saying, "Rejoice!" So they came and held Him by the feet and worshiped Him. 10 Then Jesus said to them, "Do not be afraid. Go and tell My brethren to go to Galilee, and there they will see Me."

I love the phrase in verse nine, "**they came and held Him by the feet and worshiped Him.**" The place you find these women who were charged with the responsibility to be the first ones to share the good news is at the feet of Jesus worshipping Him. They were clinging to the feet that had literally fulfilled God's promise concerning Eve. They were holding the feet in their hands that had crushed the serpent's head. I

> **They were holding the feet in their hands that had crushed the serpent's head.**

get shivers up my spine just imagining this powerful scene. These women are holding to Jesus feet and He looks down and says to them, "**Go and tell My brethren to go to Galilee, and there they will see Me.**" Think of the moment Eve failed as she heard God decree over the serpent that

49

this woman you deceived will be your enemy. She will have a Seed, and He will crush your head. Now standing over these distant granddaughters of Eve, Jesus, the promised Seed, who had just crushed the serpent's head says, **"Go and tell My brethren…"**. God allowed women to be the first to declare the fulfillment of the promise. Woman was being entrusted with a message from God to share with the men. The power of the promise was operative. Things had shifted.

As we journey through the following pages, we will consider the implications of what God told the serpent in Genesis chapter three. What Daddy God told the bully sent hope deep into the core of the first woman and all women. As we continue, let's hit the fast forward button and examine the fulfillment of God's promise to Eve through the promised Seed—Jesus. How He responded to women teaches us a whole lot about God's view of women. Through the pages that lie ahead, I think I can share some insight with you that may affect the way you view women.

Chapter Four
Jesus—The Promised Seed

That . . . man . . . says women can't have as much rights as men,
`cause Christ wasn't a woman. . . where did your Christ come
from? . . . From God and a woman. Man had nothing to do with
Him. - Sojourner Truth, 1851

~

A seed contains the lives of future generations. This is true
of corn in the fields and humans on the streets. The power
to reproduce and multiply is an awesome gift bestowed by
God upon creation. Jesus is the promised Seed of Genesis
3:15. As such, He is the Seed that not only effects future
generations but all generations past, present, and future. He
is the Seed of the woman brought forth to triumph over the
kingdom of Satan. The decree that God made to the serpent
was fulfilled in Christ. He was born of a woman. Paul calls
attention to this in his letter to the Galatians.

**Gal 4:4 But when the fullness of the time had come, God
sent forth His Son, born of a woman , born under the law,
5 to redeem those who were under the law, that we might
receive the adoption as sons.**

He was the One sent to destroy the works of the devil.

1 John 3:8 He who sins is of the devil, for the devil has sinned from the beginning. For this purpose the Son of God was manifested, that He might destroy the works of the devil. 9 Whoever has been born of God does not sin, for His seed remains in him; and he cannot sin, because he has been born of God.

Have you ever considered that since Jesus is the promised Seed and His Spirit lives in you, that the promised Seed and the promise of the Seed is in you and works through you? The nature of the Seed is that it cannot sin and it always overcomes. When the Spirit of Christ in us is in charge, we always overcome and we live holy lives. It is when we listen to our fallen nature that we get into trouble. When the Seed of Christ in us is at work then the works of the devil are destroyed. We are able to trample Satan under our feet because Jesus trampled him under His feet. A little later in First John the Apostle wrote,

1 John 4:4 You are of God, little children, and have overcome them, because He who is in you is greater than he who is in the world.

Because of the power of the blood of Jesus and the Holy Spirit's presence in our lives, we are able to continue to carry out the works of Jesus in the earth. We not only are ordained for greatness, but the Spirit of the Great One lives in us. Jesus clearly taught that His followers would continue to walk in the power He walked in and would see even greater works.

John 14: 12 Most assuredly, I say to you, he who believes in Me, the works that I do he will do also; and greater works than these he will do, because I go to My Father.

This is challenging to us. This means that we can read what Jesus did and expect to do the same things and even greater. Jesus taught that His return to the Father would usher in a change that would be experienced by His followers. This change was the coming of the Holy Spirit that was poured out on Pentecost. Of special note is that it was

> **We not only are ordained for greatness, but the Spirit of the Great One lives in us.**

announced that the Spirit was to be poured out on all flesh—men and women, Jew and Gentile, free and slaves. This was absolutely radical! The following verse underscores this shift in humanity's communion with God.

Gal 3:26 For you are all sons of God through faith in Christ Jesus. 27 For as many of you as were baptized into Christ have put on Christ. 28 There is neither Jew nor Greek, there is neither slave nor free, there is neither male nor female; for you are all one in Christ Jesus. 29 And if you are Christ's, then you are Abraham's seed, and heirs according to the promise.

53

Note that our position in Christ means that we:

- are all sons.
- have all put on Christ.
- not limited by ethnic barriers.
- are all free.
- not limited by gender.
- are all one in Christ.
- are all seed of Abraham.
- all heirs of the promise made to Abraham.
- all have access to the promises rooted in the Seed.

As is clear, we are now living in a different age than people prior to Jesus first coming. He changed things for us all. Our position before God, our union with God, and our access to God are different because of what Jesus did. However, when we live with the mentality rooted in the curse and do not adjust to the fact that the curse has been broken through the redemption of Christ, we limit ourselves from experiencing the fullness of freedom and restoration that is available to us. Often, the

We will either view women through the lens of the curse or the cross.

war is over the renewing of our minds which causes us to begin seeing things through the power of the cross. We will either view women through the lens of the curse or the cross. The way we view women will inevitably affect how we treat women and/or how you live as a woman.

Jesus was perfect and sinless. How He treated women is based on the attributes and character of who He was. He had no hypocrisy whatsoever about Him, so how He behaved painted a true picture of what He believed. He lived in a time and culture where women were largely seen as chattel, mere property of men. How did He treat women? How did He behave around them? Did He include them, value them, and respect them? These questions and their answers are important.

Jesus was radical in His approach to women. His actions toward women and on behalf of women were nothing short of revolutionary. He was certainly viewed by the religious leaders of His day as being unorthodox, unlearned, and downright heretical. He ministered to a woman who had an issue of blood. Ceremonially, she was unclean and therefore off limits for a holy man to be near. He allowed women to travel with Him and His disciples which definitely was outside the acceptable traditions of His day. Some of those who traveled with Him were women who were formerly demonized and unclean due to disease. He even accepted provisions from them. The following passage allows us to peer into the ministry of Jesus.

Luke 8:1 Now it came to pass, afterward, that He went through every city and village, preaching and bringing the glad tidings of the kingdom of God. And the twelve were with Him, 2 and certain women who had been healed of

evil spirits and infirmities — Mary called Magdalene, out of whom had come seven demons, 3 and Joanna the wife of Chuza, Herod's steward, and Susanna, and many others who provided for Him from their substance.

The church is now the expression of Christ's body in the earth today. Therefore, it seems it would be pleasing to the Father for His Son's body, the church, to be ministered to in the same loving way that the disciples ministered to Him when He walked through villages during the days of His earthly ministry.

> **If women ministered to His literal body while He was here, why should it seem strange for them to minister to His spiritual body, the church?**

In the above passage, Jesus was accompanied and ministered to by a group of women who had experienced His life changing touch on their lives. If women ministered to His literal body while He was here, why should it seem strange for them to minister to His spiritual body, the church? He defied the mindsets of His day by breaking with the common thinking about the role of women.

Jesus often taught in public places with women present. This was against the teaching of the religious teachers of His time. The *Mishnah* taught men that "He who talks much with womankind brings evil upon himself."[7] In Samaria, Jesus talked with a woman who was a moral outcast in her community. He even taught her concerning the truths of Scripture. He did not chastise her for evangelizing her community. All of this was out of bounds for His day. He forgave a woman caught in adultery and refused to condemn her. Through a word of wisdom from God, He stopped the woman from being executed at the hands of angry men. It was an intense occasion, and He put Himself in harm's way to do what He did. By the way, where was the man that committed adultery with her? Tells us something about the times, doesn't it? Believe it or not, women being stoned in public is still practiced today. It is reportedly in epidemic proportions in Iran. The following quote reveals the modern day shocking practice.

> The stoning of women is one of the more savage, and revealing aspects of the mullahs' rule in Iran. This vicious punishment of women is without precedent in Iran's recent history. Since the inception of the mullahs' rule, hundreds of women of various ages have been and continue to be stoned to death throughout Iran.[8]

The vicious stonings mentioned above involve digging a hole in the ground, burying the victim to the waist and then pelting them with stones to the upper torso and head until they are dead. This shows us what happens when religious mentalities refuse to become transformed to the truths that Jesus taught.

Jesus went to the house where a little girl had died and ministered to her though others would view His actions as making Him unclean. On another occasion, He ministered deliverance and then healing to a woman and referred to her as a daughter of Abraham. In doing this, He placed honor and bestowed blessing upon her. Sons were used to hearing such expressions but not daughters. Jesus recognized their value and included them in God's covenant promises.

He also allowed Gentile women to speak to Him, and He spoke to them in return. He allowed a woman who was known as a prostitute to kiss His feet and rub them with her hair. He did this while religious men watched and condemned Him. He did not allow their wrong mindsets to keep Him from honoring the repentant woman in the presence of other men. He even prophesied that she would continually be honored for what she did—and she has been. Two of His closest friends were Mary and Martha. He often ate with them at their house and allowed Mary to sit at His feet as He taught about His Father. Jesus kept company and would sit in a circle and talk with men and women. In Mark 3, He called them His brothers and sisters.

Mark 3:34 And He looked around in a circle at those who sat about Him, and said, "Here are My mother and My brothers! 35 For whoever does the will of God is My brother and My sister and mother."

Over and over again, Jesus stood against the cultural beliefs about women and walked contrary to them. He refused to walk to the drum beat His culture played. He confronted the hypocrisy in men, overthrew their traditions,

Women felt safe with Jesus.

and demonstrated love and respect to women. He came to restore culture, raise the standard, and correct abuses. He touched the lives of women. He preached to them. He ministered to them. He expressed love to them. He cared for them. He esteemed them. He saw them as having value. He literally risked His life in order to express value to women and ultimately gave His life to redeem us all.

Women received from Jesus what God intended them to receive from men—love, honor, respect, value, and acceptance. Women felt safe with Jesus. They felt whole. To other men of His day, women were more often than not, objects of beauty for sexual pleasure or free labor. Jesus recognized that there was more to a woman than outward beauty and manual labor.

As Jesus hung on the cross bearing the reproach of humanity's sin, hearing the curses of religious men filled with hatred toward Him, and suffering unbearable pain, He could look down from the cross and see the faces of women who never left Him. Eve's daughters stayed in the shadow of the cross until the promise was fulfilled. They were the last to hear Him speak before He died and the first to hear Him speak after He arose.

As I mentioned earlier, when He arose from the dead, He first appeared to women. It was a woman He first charged to share the good news that He was risen from the dead. How fitting that a daughter of Eve be the first to declare the fulfillment of the prophetic declaration that Father God made to the serpent.

It is clear in reading through the New Testament that the men who followed Jesus learned to give honor to their wives and to recognize the value of women. After Jesus' ascension, both men and women were meeting and praying together in the upper room. Both men and women were filled with the Holy Spirit on the Day of

> **How fitting that a daughter of Eve be the first to declare the fulfillment of the prophetic declaration that Father God made to the serpent.**

Pentecost. Peter preached that the Spirit was being poured out on all flesh (men and women) and sons and daughters and men and women slaves would prophesy. *This was radical!* The Apostle Paul in writing to the believers in Ephesus taught the men to love their wives in the same way that Christ loved the church. He gave Himself for her. This sacrificial and self-denying love was a bold initiative for the men who lived in the first century. When writing to the church in Corinth, Paul had to clear up a lot of misunderstanding about the role of women and spiritual gifts. The obvious thing that seems to always be overlooked is the fact that the church at Corinth had certainly been taught that men and women were to participate in worship together. This was also radical.

It is important for you to understand that there are controversial texts in the New Testament that seem to indicate that a woman is never to speak in church

> **The serpent worked through a woman to birth sin, and God worked through a woman to birth a Savior.**

and she is never to exercise authority in a male context. It is also important to realize that there are passages in the New Testament that seem to indicate that women did the things that other passages forbid. I encourage you to remember as I mentioned earlier in this chapter, that whatever you read in the New Testament must square with the actions and teachings of Jesus Himself.

The restoration of the voice of woman is consistent with what Jesus did and what God says. It is just like God to reverse what the serpent started. The serpent worked through a woman to birth sin, and God worked through a woman to birth a Savior. He told the serpent that One would be born to redeem fallen man, and He reminded ancient Israel often of their promised savior who would come. This was fulfilled by the crucifixion of Jesus.

Isaiah 7:14 Therefore the Lord Himself will give you a sign: Behold, the virgin shall conceive and bear a Son, and shall call His name Immanuel.

What an amazing story the birth of Christ is! What an awesome event it was when the Holy Spirit who had hovered over the waters at the beginning of creation began to hover over the womb of a young virgin named Mary! What a miracle it was when God created in her womb, the Christ child! Mystery of mysteries, that Eternal God took upon Himself the form of a man. The Second Person of the Godhead, God the Son, became Jesus of Nazareth. He came through the womb of a woman. God's Seed in the Woman's womb became the answer to all the problems caused by humanity's sin. If He used a woman to literally bear His Only Begotten Son, then why does it seem so strange that He would use a woman to bear the message about His Only Begotten Son?

The Gospel always takes a culture up when it is properly understood and applied. Women in the first century were kept in the cultural cellar, but Jesus' loving actions and revolutionary teaching started bringing them up and out. Jesus' power to change culture and lift women into their destiny is still at work today!

Chapter Five
The Real Issue Between the Sexes

Women belong in the house... and the Senate. —*Author Unknown*

~

In the third chapter of Genesis, we find the record of the infamous bite that changed the world. It chronicles for us the "BIG MISTAKE" that started a long string of bad news events for humankind. It was the moment in human history that created a crisis for women. What happened then is still sending shockwaves and causing trouble today around the world. Before that moment, the world was a perfect and harmonious world. Since that moment there has been a war waging for the souls of humankind and a war waging between the sexes.

Can you imagine what it would have been like to have witnessed the drama of Genesis three in real time? We can only read about it and then imagine what it would have been like……

- Somehow Satan influences the serpent.
- The serpent shows up in the garden.
- Eve dialogs with the serpent.
- She eats a piece of the fruit from the tree of the knowledge of good and evil.

- She gives the fruit to Adam.
- He eats along with her.
- As they swallow, something happens.
- They feel a strange sensation.
- Something is wrong.
- They had never felt this feeling before.
- They sense the feeling of being in trouble.
- This was a brand new but terrifying experience.
- Fear introduced itself to them.
- They realized they were naked.
- Self awareness kicked in.
- They viewed each other differently for the first time.
- They became suspicious.
- The weight of guilt settled in their souls.
- The knowledge of evil came to stay.
- They felt condemned.
- The reality of judgment sent shockwaves of terror into their lives.

Up to that moment they enjoyed such unity and oneness that the idea of otherness was foreign to them. Individuality took over their consciousness. They shifted from corporate to private thinking. The first thoughts of self-protection filled their minds. For the first time they consider each other a threat. All these new and terrible feelings flooded their beings. They only had each other--so they ran--they ran together. They hid. They never had considered such a thing before. They had never entertained the idea of not wanting to be found or seen or heard. Suspicion, fear, blame, and the desire to hide all flooded their minds. Their view of God was changed in that moment.

Now they were afraid.
Afraid of God.
Afraid of what God would do.
Afraid of what would happen to them.
Another terrifying thing happened.
They heard God calling for them.
What would they do?
It was always joyful before when they heard His voice--but now things had changed.
They had failed God.
They had failed themselves.
They had ignored the one thing He had told them not to do.
Adam is thinking, "Why did I listen to her? "
Eve is thinking, "Why did I believe the serpent?"
As Father God drew near, they stepped out before Him in their fig-leaf attire. It was a high-noon showdown with God, and they knew who was going to win.
"Why are you hiding?" God asks.
"We were naked and afraid," Adam replies.

"Who told you that you were naked? You ate of the tree, didn't you?" God tightens the net.

"The woman you gave me--she gave it to me--and I ate," Adam quickly and defensively replied.

"The serpent told me to do it," Eve replied.

The serpent is still saying things to women and to men about each other that are not true.

This is the nature of sin—it is very deceptive! The real issue between men and women boils down to one little three letter word that begins with an "s"—SIN. Yes, as popular as it is to practice it, and as unpopular as it is to believe in it, I do believe the basic human dilemma is the issue of sin. I unapologetically believe that the account of Adam and Eve as recorded in the biblical record is accurate, literal, and inspired of God. I discount the notion that the Bible is mere mythology that offers an uneducated view of the origin of civilization. When we reduce the Bible, our guidebook to life, to a myth, we are left with only fairy tales and fantasies. The accusations of the extreme liberals are that the Bible is myth and Christian men are all misguided misogynists (a fancy word for woman haters).

> **We need truth so that we can have freedom.**

We need truth so that we can have freedom. Thank God for imagination, but we need revelation. The book of Genesis is foundational to all we believe. It is the revelation that has been given to us concerning who God is and who we are. Wrong views of Genesis end up making monkeys out of men. Certainly monkeys are in the Genesis account of creation along with all the other beasts, but man and woman occupy the spotlight of God's sixth day creative activity. They were created in the image of God and endowed with authority and dominion as God's regents to rule and reign in the realm of Earth for their Father's glory. To make man less is to make him a beast. To make him more is to make him a "god". Man and woman are at the top of all creation, just under God Himself. We must not exalt humanity into godhood, and we must not reduce humanity into beasthood. We must see humanity through the lens of Scripture.

At the dawn of civilization in the paradise God made for man called Eden, something happened. That *something* created a wound in the soul of man and a wound in the soul of woman. For the most part, humanity has never been healed from that *something* that happened.

That *something* was sin.
That *something* was a snakebite to the soul.
That *something* was a barrier built.
That *something* was a lie swallowed.
That *something* was a distrust born.
That *something* put a doubt into man's spiritual DNA toward woman.

By understanding what happened in Eden and what God has done in response, there can be healing of the wounds that have festered in the souls of men and women since the Fall.

Something was left in Eden that could not leave.
Something was carried out that could not stay.
The flaming swords that guarded Eden can now be lowered through the power of the cross of Christ.
That something left in Eden can now be restored.
That something carried from Eden can now be exposed.

> **What you believe about the Fall of man determines the direction that your theology is going to take.**

Our Christian history is rooted in a belief that something bad happened to the entire human race due the disobedience of Adam and Eve in the Garden of Eden. Through the action of eating the forbidden fruit from the Tree of the Knowledge of Good and Evil, the first couple steered the whole human family away from God. What you believe about the Fall of man determines the direction that your theology is going to take. Theology is the study about God. In other words, it's what you believe about God. What you really believe about who God is can be found rooted in who you believe man and woman to be. It is somewhat cyclical, but what you believe about God reflects what you really believe about man—and–what you believe about man reflects what you really believe about God. Don't worry, we won't stay on this theological treadmill long, but it is important. Both the attributes of God and the attributes of man are very important in forming a person's belief system.

If a child is taught that they can do no wrong (no sinful nature), inevitably they will be irresponsible and painfully prideful. If a child is taught that there is no way of redemption when they do wrong (fatalism), inevitably they will become hopeless and depressed or wild and reckless or both. I believe the Bible clearly teaches that man and woman are sinners whom God loves so much that He sent His only begotten Son Jesus to die to set them free. The cross was necessary because of the fact of man's sinful nature.

Those, who like 17th century philosopher John Locke, say that all of humanity is born *Tabula Rasa* (a clean slate), deny the fact that humanity is under the curse of sin and that we live in a fallen world. Locke theorized that each of us arrive with a blank mental slate that becomes filled only through sensory experiences. This theory reduces man's responses to his environment and to his personal history. It fails to take into account the history that was genetically passed on to him through his parents. Certainly, we are taught our personal history after we are born, but to say we have no history before we were born is to deny the very parents who gave us birth. It is a reversion to the stork story that we were just dropped off one day from who knows where. I believe the Bible teaches that we arrive here with a nature predisposed toward sin. That nature was passed to us through our parents who received it from their parents, who received it from – well, ultimately—from Adam and Eve. The gospel (good news) is that Jesus came to die for us and through the power of the Holy Spirit give us a new nature that is more powerful than the old one we received from Adam. The Apostle Paul states it this way in the letter he wrote to believers in Rome:

Rom 5:18 Therefore, as through one man's offense judgment came to all men, resulting in condemnation, even so through one Man's righteous act the free gift came to all men, resulting in justification of life. 19 For as by one man's disobedience many were made sinners, so also by one Man's obedience many will be made righteous.

As many preachers from many pulpits have said, "The heart of the problem is the problem of the heart." Humanity has a heart problem. This problem is called sin. Though sin is a word seen nowadays to be a relic of a less enlightened era, *sin* is still the problem and still the one thing that separates humanity from God.

Your belief about sin will determine what you really believe about salvation. I was recently reading a book entitled, *The Christian and The Pharisee*. This wonderful book chronicles a series of letters written back and forth between Dr. R.T. Kendall and Rabbi David Rosen in which they debate the road to Heaven. In one of Dr. Kendall's letters to Rabbi Rosen, he addressed the issue of the Fall of man.

"So I am curious to know, since you aver that people today are born as Adam and Eve were created before the Fall, why is it always the case – no exceptions – that people sin and die? Surely, David, if you are correct, somebody one day among the billions of people that have been born would by now have proved your thesis that people are born intrinsically good. But all end up sinning, and all die. The one exception: Yeshua (Jesus), who later raised to life for our justification (Rom. 4:25)."

This is why the New Testament points to what came to be known as the doctrine of original sin, which you say you do not accept. You will know that Augustine put the position like this:

Posse pacare (able to sin) – that is, Adam and Eve before the Fall.

Non posse non pecare (not able not to sin) – that is, people after the Fall.

Posse non pecare (able not to sin) – that is, those who have faith in Christ.

Non posse pecare (not able to sin) – that is, once we are in Heaven.

71

Even if you lay aside Augustine and the New Testament, I would have thought that empirical evidence for people's predictability – they always sin sooner or later – suggests they must have been born with the propensity to sin. Where did this proclivity come from?"[9]

Dr. Kendall's question, *"Where did this proclivity come from?"* must be answered correctly for us to have the right worldview. I believe that Augustine's statements are biblically correct and provide us a wonderfully accurate synopsis of the drama of God's redemption for fallen

> **Your belief about sin will determine what you really believe about salvation.**

humanity. Man, apart from the redemptive intervention of God, is unable to save himself from his own sinfulness. The love in Father God's heart moved Him to come in the form of a man, live a sinless life (which Adam and Eve failed to do), die a sacrificial death on behalf of fallen man, and conquer death itself through the resurrection. After which, He poured out upon those believing in Christ His Holy Spirit as a gift to seal the deal. Wow! This is really good news. Think about it:

1. Perfect God with a perfect man and woman who were given the ability to choose to commit sin.
2. Disobedient man and woman lose the ability to live in dominion over sin.

3. Perfect God became Perfect Man to redeem fallen man and woman and restore their ability to live in dominion over sin.
4. Perfect man and perfect woman without the ability to commit sin living eternally with Perfect God.

This brings us to the point at hand, and a major point of this entire book – the issue of the curse and what God intended through what He said to the serpent and to Adam and Eve on that first occasion when they "blew" it.

There is no denying that sin brought with it a curse upon humanity. What is a curse? Think in terms of its opposite--- a blessing. A curse is what a blessing is not. The curse is simply the manifested consequence of sin. The manifestations of sin are death, disease, destruction, and the increase of more evil. Even sin reproduces after its own kind. Evidence of this is seen in family lines. The sin of the father is passed on to the children and so forth (Exodus 20:4-6). Up until the moment when Adam and Eve entered into sin through their disobedience, they had never experienced sickness, discomfort, or anything less than maximum productivity and blessing. All the creation was subject to them and responded positively to them. The Bible teaches us that the earth is groaning right now just waiting for the day when the children of God fully manifest their God ordained destiny once again (Romans 8:22).

The entry of sin into the human race created a negative shift in the earth. Think with me about those moments when God came to the Garden of Eden after the Fall. Let's examine His responses. I believe we can catch some clear glimpses of the motivations and plans that fill the heart of God for humanity by investigating His response to Adam, Eve, and the serpent. I am amazed by what I have discovered in this well-known text, especially in regard to what God had to say to the serpent who beguiled His beloved daughter Eve ultimately leading to her downfall and that of His precious son Adam.

Chapter Six
Daddy's Girl & the Bully

A lie gets halfway around the world before the truth has a chance to get its pants on. - Sir Winston Churchill

~

Women are used to hearing about the prowess and power of a man. They also hear a lot of what men have to say about women. It is usually in relation to their curves, their hair, or their outfits. When is the last time you heard a man speak about the wisdom of a woman, the leadership skills of a woman, or the anointing on a woman's life? However, when the subjects of deception or seduction come up, it is almost always the woman who gets picked to be in the analogy. Sure, Eve was first deceived, but how long do her daughters have to pay for it?

We tend to let men off the hook. David committed adultery with Bathsheba, but what was she doing bathing where he could watch? The conclusion is that poor King David was pulled into a web spun by a seductive woman. This kind of thinking is not as uncommon as it ought to be. Are there seductive women? Yes, but should all women carry the blame for the few? Some of our cultural mentalities have blinded us to the truth. We have strongholds built into our minds that need dismantled by the power of God's truth.

These strongholds have produced a widespread lack of respect and honor for women. She is viewed to be in the basement of God's plans for the future. The penthouse is reserved for the men.

Women have been pushed, shoved, held back, oppressed, and denied honor and respect since Eve's trip out of Eden.

> **Sure, Eve was first deceived, but how long do her daughters have to pay for it?**

The daughters of Eve have had to face bullies all of their lives. In many countries, there is an outright war on women. Consider this excerpt from an article about the war against women in the Basra area of Iraq where insurgents are rising up against the threat of a true democracy being established.

Across Iraq, a bloody and relentless oppression of women has taken hold. Many women had their heads shaved for refusing to wear a scarf or have been stoned in the street for wearing make-up. Others have been kidnapped and murdered for crimes that are being labeled simply as "inappropriate behavior". The insurrection against the fragile and barely functioning state has left the country prey to extremists whose notion of freedom does not extend to women.[10]

In Saudi Arabia, women are not allowed to drive. They can own a car, but they cannot drive it. If allowed to drive they might have contact with men working as gas station attendants or male officers at security checkpoints. The nation's adherence to a very strict Islamic worldview prohibits women from virtually all actions that would cause them to be around men who are not relatives. Therefore to a large degree, they are isolated to their homes. One Saudi

> **One Saudi woman said that the climate is like that in which Rosa Parks finally refused to move to the back of the bus.**

woman said that the climate is like that in which Rosa Parks finally refused to move to the back of the bus.[11]

In Africa, there are locations where tribal beliefs allow a man to have multiple wives. Women are also beaten, violently caned, stabbed, and marital rape is practiced regularly. One article gives a snapshot of what some Muslim women in the coastal area of Kenya, East Africa face:

> Often, upon the death of their spouses, women are violently chased away from their matrimonial homes, penniless and without any material wealth to their credit.[12]

I recently returned from a trip to Tanzania, East Africa, where I shared a message on the restoration of women. It was so awesome to see the tears streaming down the faces of the women and the Spirit of God moving upon the hearts of the men. Many of the men in the churches there are beginning to walk in the revelation of woman's restoration. We need to pray that this will begin to influence the tribal culture there. Among the Massai tribal group in Tanzania and Kenya, many of the men have multiple wives which they acquire by trading cattle for them. We drove by one village where we were shown a cluster of huts that belonged to a man who had 22 wives. These wives were a sign of his wealth and power in the community. Women are seen as the possessions of men.

There are still many places in India where women are not allowed to eat at the table with men. I have been there and experienced this first hand. Segregation of the sexes is still alive and thriving. Certainly there is a place for modesty and for appropriate relating to the opposite sex, but to virtually ban all social interaction is primitive and unbiblical.

Some women are definitely more oppressed than others and fortunately there are some who enjoy the sweet taste of freedom. But millions of women in these modern times still struggle with being able to express themselves and step into their destinies. One out of every three women in the world has been beaten, coerced into sex, or abused in some way during their lifetimes. Each year in the United States, estimates indicate that there are between one and three million instances of domestic violence committed against women by their husbands, boyfriends, or former partners. This environment of oppression is reality for many women.

Trapped!
Suffocated!
Silenced!
Ignored!
Intimidated!

These are words that describe how many women feel in their lives, marriages, churches, and culture. How they respond to these feelings vary. The pain is real when a wife in not allowed to voice her opinion on any subject that is considered vital or important. The pain is real when women sit in churches where their voices cannot be used to pray, speak, or teach. The pain is real when women are overlooked for promotions in the workplace where they have proven themselves more capable than many of their male counterparts. Yet, they watch as men who arrived after they did earn more and are elevated sooner. The pain is real when the religious beliefs of a woman's husband forbid her to show her face in public, speak in public, or even eat at the same table when men are present. Novelist Fannie Hurst summed up the feelings of many women when she said, *"A woman has to be twice as good as a man to go half as far."*[13]

Most women have been bullied at some point in their lives. There are overbearing husbands, harassing employers, and some self-appointed men on a mission who frequently remind women that their status is inferior to men. Many women have been taught that their place is to be one of silence. As a result they remain an unheard voice, held back by the blindness and ignorance of the culture that has been imposed upon them. In a submission they assume is without options, they refuse to speak. To them destiny simply means, "Where I already am—what I already have." They feel locked into a way of life that can never change. Is this the way God intended it to be when He made a woman? Does her life have significance apart from the life of a man? Is she never to have a place where she is sought for counsel? Should her voice ever carry the weight of authority that a man's voice carries? Should her voice ever outweigh the voice of a man? This fallen world we live in with all of its sin and ignorance has caused many women to live without knowing why they were created. God's Word has much to say about the destiny of a woman.

It is time for the silence to be broken. Ladies, your Father in heaven has said some things that will encourage you as women. He prophesied that you would be a weapon in His hand used to defeat Satan (Genesis 3:15).

Chapter Seven
Daddy God & His Warrior Girls

*Sure God created man before woman. But then you always make
a rough draft before the final masterpiece. –Author Unknown*

~

From the beginning, it was ordained that daddies and
daughters were to have a special relationship. After all,
Daddy God made the first daughter and had the honor of
escorting her to the first man. Fathers still have the honor
today of presenting their daughters to the man who is to
become her husband. I am the proud father of four children
and nestled in the midst of my three sons is my only
daughter. I must admit that my heart has a soft spot for my
little girl who just turned 21. Unless there is major
dysfunction in a home, Daddy always takes care of his girls.
He is her protector until another man takes her to be his
bride and even then Daddy stands ready to help her any
way he can. It is sad when a little girl is abused by her dad.
Even in our American culture, it is estimated that two out of
every ten girls will be sexually abused by their thirteenth
birthday.[14] This is contrary to nature and the way God
intended it to be. Thank God for girls with loving daddies!

My mother washed her daddy's feet every night from the
time she was five years old until the day she married at the

age of seventeen. Each afternoon, she would go outside in the backyard where she would drop a bucket into the hand-

> **Daddy God made the first daughter and had the honor of escorting her to the first man.**

dug well and then pull it up filled with water. She would carry the water into the house where she would fill a basin. Later that night, she would bring the basin into her parent's bedroom. She would kneel down in front of where her daddy was seated and lift his feet from the floor and gently place them down into the basin of water. With a cloth in one hand and soap in the other, she would wash the day's dirt from her daddy's feet. She would rinse them, massage them, and then dry them off with a towel. My granddad looked forward to this nightly routine.

Don't think this cruel. Years earlier when he was young, my granddad had been in an accident. A bulldozer had flipped over and crushed his hip. He was crippled on one side and walked with a severe limp with the aid of a walking cane. It was not easy for him to bathe. In those days, the family took their baths outside under a makeshift shower. They would draw a bucket of water out of the well and empty it into a suspended bucket with holes punched in its bottom. The water sifted through the holes creating a shower. The family became adept at taking a one bucket cold shower. For Granddad, this was not easy to do, so he relished the footbaths my mom gave him. Had she been forced to do this, it would have been different. She did it out of love. She loved her daddy and he loved her.

A few years after she married my dad, her dad died. Across those thousands of nights, my mom had showed her daddy she loved him. Their hearts were bonded in an unusual way. Granddad would have done anything for her. He loved his girl. In his hardship, he would occasionally buy her a special gift. Daddies are supposed to be that way toward their girls. They love and protect their little girls. Shame on those who don't!

Since the sun set in Eden on the day humanity fell, Daddy God has been working to reverse what happened to His son and daughter—Adam and Eve. The enemy came and attacked His girl, and she fell for his trick. As every good daddy would do, her Daddy stepped in to help. God has a special place in His heart for His girls. Of course, His nemesis—Satan—hates what God loves. There is no denying that women have been the target of the enemy down through the ages. Satan has worked overtime to subjugate and exploit women. He still desires to overthrow God's plans and disprove God's Word. He hates God and God's Word, and therefore he attacks them with all the power of darkness he can muster.

This explains in part his special hatred of women. Satan is the ultimate misogynist, the woman hater of all woman haters. God told him from the beginning—I am going to use a woman as a weapon in My hand to overthrow you. God decreed that through the woman a child would be brought forth whose heel would crush the serpent's head. So, as we would expect, Satan is working in the opposite spirit against this prophecy. As a result you often see women in situations where they are under someone's heel. The domination of women by men is a prime example. Behind every mistreatment of woman, Satan stands in the shadows gloating. Around the world mistreatment of women is still a major issue. We have fought heated battles over it here in the wonderful U.S.A. as I will discuss later on. Understanding the root of it all will give us insight concerning the fruit of it all.

Let's read again the passage in question.

Gen 3:15 And I will put enmity
Between you and the woman,
And between your seed and her Seed;
He shall bruise your head,
And you shall bruise His heel."

Theologians refer to Genesis 3:15 as the *protoevangelium*. This is a fancy scholarly word that simply means "the first mention of the Gospel." Clearly, this passage prophetically pictures the coming of Jesus, His death on the cross, and His glorious victory over sin, death, and Satan. The verse opens the window to a future occasion when the powers of the serpent would be crushed under the heel of the offspring of the woman.

All of my ministerial life, I have focused on the last part of verse fifteen, **"He shall bruise your head, And you shall bruise His heel."** Of course, the last part is the most important part in the big scheme of things. We all know that it was Jesus who fulfilled this prophecy. He is the ultimate snake head crusher. However, this past spring, I found myself riveted upon the first part of verse fifteen. I had read it hundreds of time, but suddenly I was seeing the text in a new way. I was preparing a message for Mother's Day and was thinking of Eve as the first mother and the *mother of all living* which is the meaning of the name Adam gave her after they sinned and were removed from Eden. I began thinking about the curse and how Eve must have felt. Then I began thinking about what God said to the serpent and how that must have affected Eve.

Think about what God said to the serpent,

**And I will put enmity
Between you and the woman…**

Can you imagine what Eve must have been feeling at the moment that God spoke these words to the serpent? Set your mind to see the context of Genesis 3:15. Eve had just been subtly deceived by the serpent. She had given away the Garden of Eden. Her husband had been complicit with her. She had just experienced a flood of negative emotions, all of which, she had never experienced before. She was overcome with guilt—the weight of the judgment of sin was now upon her. She was filled with fear. She realized that she had disobeyed God. She was struggling with grief over what she had done. She now knew that there were forces working against her to destroy her. Certainly, she was also dealing with anger at herself, at the serpent, and possibly Adam.

Eve had one more big case of head-hanging shame.
Guilt had gripped her conscience for the first time.
Fear made its grand first entrance into her heart.
Rejection wrapped itself around her mind.
She certainly felt like a debilitated failure.
Utter hopelessness overloaded her soul.
She had blown it big time.
The honeymoon ended.
The party was over.
It was all over!
No more Eden!

All of these particular emotional encounters were first time experiences for Eve. She had been created to stand at her husband's side. The two of them had been given authority and dominion over the whole creative order on earth. They had been entrusted with the assignment to be fruitful and to fill the earth with children.

Before child one was ever born, it was over!
The dreams of their future were spoiled.
The life—that could have been— could no longer be.

We have all felt the stinging, nagging, weight of personal failure. We all know what shame does to our way of thinking. We all have bowed the knee to fear. We all have struggled with the grief that comes when we mess things up. It's like the whole world stops, stares at you, points its finger at you, condemns you, and blames you for all its ills. This was the pain in Eve's soul as she heard God begin speaking to the serpent. If ever someone messed up, she did! If someone ever needed encouragement, she did! Hear what God said to Eve as He spoke to the serpent. Yes. You heard me right. I believe that Eve received a powerful message through what Father God said to the serpent. Haven't you ever gotten a revelation from God through what He said to someone else? This happens all the time when a preacher preaches. Those listening get the benefits of the revelation the preacher received from God.

With her heart sagging in the pain of failure, Eve hears the voice of God pronouncing a curse upon the serpent. In the middle of the decree of the serpent's curse, Eve received an

87

incredible word of life and blessing. What an astounding statement echoes from the heart of God. **"And I will put enmity between you and the woman."**

In addressing the serpent, Father still had His daughter on His mind. I imagine this as a Father stepping in between His daughter and the bully who has dishonored her. Note that God says that *He* would be the One Who would put enmity between the serpent and the woman. It's like God is saying,

> **In the middle of the decree of the serpent's curse, Eve received an incredible word of life and blessing.**

"Serpent, you will regret the day you did this to my daughter. This will not happen again! From now on, the woman will be your enemy." Think of it—God decreed that woman would become an enemy in the Earth against the forces of the serpent. The word "put" as used here means to "place or set something somewhere." What is being placed? Enmity! Enmity is the Hebrew word *'eybah*. It is a noun which means hostility, animosity, or ill will.[15] Where is it being placed? Between the Serpent and the Woman!

In the book of Ezekiel, the word is translated as "old hatred" and "ancient hatred" (Ezk.25:15; 35:5). Numbers 35:21 describes a situation where one person strikes another person in enmity which results in death and states that this is murder. For sure, the word implies that God Himself was going to put a great distaste in the mouth of the woman toward the serpent. She would hate him, have ill will toward him, and seek to do him in. From this decree an ancient hatred has developed between the woman and the serpent. History is replete with various ways the serpent has worked to keep the status of women in a place of degradation, devaluing, and destruction.

Now it may be asked, "Was God putting this enmity in the serpent toward the woman or in the woman toward the serpent?" The serpent, obviously, already had it in for the woman. The rest of biblical revelation sheds light on the fact that it was Satan who was working through the serpent. Consider the following passage from the book of Revelation that describes the lineage of the Devil.

Rev 12:9 So the great dragon was cast out, that serpent of old, called the Devil and Satan, who deceives the whole world; he was cast to the earth, and his angels were cast out with him.

Here he is called, *the serpent of old.* He is said to be the one *who deceives the whole world.*

The Apostle Paul was concerned that the people whom he had led to the Lord in Corinth in danger of being deceived. He implies that a spirit of deception is at work through false teachers to seduce them away from their bridegroom, Jesus, just as Eve had been seduced away from her bridegroom, Adam. Paul clearly draws a parallel between the spirit working through the serpent and Satan.

2 Cor 11:2 For I am jealous for you with godly jealousy. For I have betrothed you to one husband, that I may present you as a chaste virgin to Christ. 3 But I fear, lest somehow, as the serpent deceived Eve by his craftiness, so your minds may be corrupted from the simplicity that is in Christ. 4 For if he who comes preaches another Jesus whom we have not preached, or if you receive a different spirit which you have not received, or a different gospel which you have not accepted — you may well put up with it!

In addition, I dare not accuse our loving Father God of creating or placing the desire in Satan's heart to destroy Adam and Eve. Satan's desire to destroy arises out of his own fallen nature that was poisoned by his own pride in eternity past. We lay the blame on the wrong doorstep when we try to leave it at God's address.

Since Satan already had it in for the first couple, I believe the enmity God placed was in the heart of the woman toward the serpent. She was the one deceived and hoodwinked by the serpent. Therefore, God decreed that He would use the woman to be the means to birth the One who would undo the serpent. In other words, the serpent started the problem with woman and landed the first debilitating blow—but—she would rise up from her failure and become the enemy of the serpent. The promise to Eve should be claimed by all of Eve's daughters. A woman should declare, ***"I am an enemy to Satan and all the evil he stands for."*** When she declares this, she is voicing agreement with what God has already said. She is prophesying her destiny. She is speaking out of her mouth what God has put in her heart.

The fact that God decreed that the woman would be hostile toward the serpent is good news! I know God's words were first mentioned in the curse given to the serpent, but the curse upon the serpent is good news for humanity. In reality, the Lord only cursed the serpent and the ground, not the man and the woman. What He had to say to Adam and Eve had to do with how their lives would change due to the sin they had entered into. Sin brings its own result. The sin inside them changed them and caused ungodly desires to arise from their fallen nature. They came under the power of the curse of sin. God blessed His kids. They cursed themselves. God pronounced the results of what they had done.

It is a good thing when God Himself says to a person, "You are Satan's enemy!" You certainly would not want to hear the Lord testify that "You are Satan's friend!" So, it was a good thing for Eve that God decreed what He did. Can you imagine how she felt when she heard these words?

She and Adam both felt like they had it coming. They both ran and hid from God. They knew they had blown it big time, yet the first thing that happens when the Lord's ammo starts flying is the decree that from now on the woman would be a weapon in His hand against the war on Satan. The woman who had been weak in her encounter with the serpent was now decreed to be a warrior against him and his seed. Isn't this just like God? He is able to reverse things. This is what He had in mind—a plan to reverse what had just happened through the Fall of Man. The shadow of Calvary's cross prophetically fell across Eden through the words God released to the serpent. The talking head of the serpent that had seductively drawn the woman into sin would be crushed by the heel of a future Son. A son that would be carried in the womb of one of the daughters of Eve would be the one to silence the voice of the snake and restore the voice of the woman.

> **The woman who had been weak in her encounter with the serpent was now decreed to be a warrior against him and his seed.**

Please allow me to step into a little more typology with this text. In a typological sense, Eve is now represented by the Church. Adam is represented by Jesus who became the last Adam. The Church, the bride of the Last Adam, is now protected by her bridegroom. Satan is still working hard to deceive the new woman in the Earth.

However, she is the means through which the Spirit of God works to trample Satan's empire and advance the kingdom of her Kingly Husband. She is reproducing children for Him and filling the earth with His sons and daughters. She, with Him at her side, is walking the earth in dominion. This is the part of the process of the restoration of all things. She is able to walk with her heel on Satan's head. It is also a picture of what God intends in a Christian marriage--a man and a woman walking together in power and authority. The man loves the woman sacrificially, and the woman respects the man from which she came.

I encourage you women warriors to personalize this decree of the Lord over your life and the lives of your children. Pray it! Stand on it! Use it as a weapon in your hand. You can use it to pray something like the following:

"I am a warrior! The Lord Himself decreed that I am to be an enemy of Satan. I take my stand against all the work of the serpent against my life and the lives of my seed. I hold to the promise of God's Word that I will be used of Him to see the empire of evil toppled. My seed, through the power of Jesus Christ, will trample the enemy under their feet! My seed and I are endowed with the destiny to oppose and overcome the evil that rises up against us. I am a warrior. I am my heavenly Father's daughter. His kingdom is being established in me and through me, in my seed and through my seed. The victory is assured in me and in my seed. The enemy must flee in Jesus name. Amen!"

Wow! That felt good, didn't it? It should have. It is part of who you have been called and created to be—a warrior. It agrees with the distant memory of Eve that lingers in your spiritual DNA. Dear Sister in Christ, You are a warrior! In chapter fifteen, *The Power of A Mother's Decree*, we will look at how women can stand in the gap for their children on the basis of this word God spoke in Eve's hearing. Keep reading. Get ready! Arm yourself with the weapon of this word and fight! As we shall see, women are much tougher than most men realize.

Chapter Eight
The Tender-Tough Ones

A woman is like a tea bag - you never know how strong she is until she gets in hot water. - *Eleanor Roosevelt*

~

If God can't find a man to do it, He'll use a woman! We've all heard this statement, but what is really being said when it is used?

- God prefers men?
- Women are second rate?
- If desperate, God will use a woman?
- Women are God's last resort?
- Because of His great power, God can use anything to accomplish His purposes--even a woman?

Some men concede that if God could speak to Balaam through a donkey, then its possible God could speak through a woman. This arrogant, self-aggrandizing attitude among men reveals that we have a core problem in respecting and honoring women. We men find it hard to think that maybe, just maybe, there are times when God prefers to use a woman. Maybe there are times when a woman is better than a man. Why do we men struggle? I am not saying all men--but let's say a "bunch" of men struggle with this. Why? Why do men have an innate predisposition to distrust the voice of women?

We often:
- look down on women.
- struggle with feeling superior.
- act as if we are superior.
- neglect and ignore what women have to say.
- are oblivious to how women really feel.
- ignore the evidence of what God has placed in a woman's life and what God does through a woman's life.

These proposed stereotypical statements are not without substance. They can be documented historically, biblically--and if most men were painfully honest--personally. Women are frequently viewed by men as being weak, whiney, and wimpy.

Subconsciously, sometimes men theologically surmise the following:

"Since Eve listened to the snake and took the first bite--she proved that women are weak and cannot be trusted in making important decisions. Because of her failure, God banished her to the bench and looks only to His sons to do what needs to be done on Earth. The woman comes in handy in providing more sons to lead the next generation. Therefore, women are to serve men, keep them happy, have their kids, and keep their mouths shut."

While this may be mildly overstated, it does represent a sub-conscious train of thought that rests in the belief system in the minds of many men and women of our culture. It is getting better. The situation for women is slowly improving, but the Bible may say more about the dignity, beauty, wonder, and strength of women than we may have been willing to hear. Sadly, there are women around the world and across the street who continue to be exploited and tormented by men who have a low regard for the mystery and wonder of a woman. To them, she is mere property like a car or condominium. She is treated as a slave and has fewer rights than any man, whether friend or foe. She is ignored, neglected, mistreated, and excluded in the world of men that surround her.

According to a United Nations Report, women constitute half the world's population, perform nearly two-thirds of its work hours, receive one-tenth of the world's income and own less than one-hundredth of the world's property. The room of history has been a little crowded and noisy with faces and voices working overtime to disparage the image of women. God's truth sheds light and gives hope to women in their struggle to regain the place forfeited in Eden.

> **While man did nothing, God made a woman.**

It's time this mentality is moved out of the way so humanity can move on with the program. While man did nothing, God made a woman. God worked while Adam rested. Afterward, Adam was the beneficiary of what God had made. Man was out of it when God created woman and in a way we men are still in the dark about the creature called "woman." Since the dawn of man and woman's first days together on this beautiful planet, war has existed against the purposes of God for women. The common perspective of men down through the centuries has placed women in a substandard position as a human being. She has been degraded, humiliated, exploited, and prostituted against her will by domineering men which are all contrary to God's desires. Woman is so valued by the Lord that He chose her to describe His own relationship with His church. He looks at His church and sees His bride. She is loved and cherished by Him. She has been made to be the recipient of His intoxicating love. He has made her His treasure. He is working even now preparing a place for her and making plans for the gala of all galas which will take place at His wedding banquet prepared for His bride.

Let's face it. Men and women are different. We've been taught that women are from Venus, and men are from Mars. I think those planets are far too close together to be used for such an analogy. They are still in the same galaxy. The battle of the sexes didn't begin yesterday. It began with Eden's first bite. Maybe before. Adam probably pondered the complexity of Eve from the beginning. Maybe he was pondering when she was eating and that's what got him in trouble. See, there I go. I'm thinking like a man. I'm giving Adam an "out" because Eve was so complicated. Typical macho technique. I'm sorry. I repent. I, like the rest of the men on earth, need to be healed.

Sexual identity is an important but confusing issue in our culture. The simple *men are men* and *women are women* kind of thinking really does get confused. The gender identity debate is just another evidence that the serpent wants to confuse men and women about who God says they are and who God made them to be. Men and women each have their roles in culture and in the kingdom. There is the need for strong godly men and strong godly women. Together they are the team God created to get the job done.

Men have a hard time thinking of women as strong. I recently received a humorous email that drives home a point I want to make in this chapter.[16] It's an alleged letter sent by a soldier at boot camp to Ma and Pa back home. Let me share it with you. You'll laugh. I'll make my point. We'll move on from there.

Dear Ma and Pa,

I am well. Hope you are. Tell Brother Walt and Brother Elmer the Marine Corps beats working for old man Minch by a mile. Tell them to join up quick before all of the places are filled. I was restless at first because you got to stay in bed till nearly 6 A. M. but I am getting so I like to sleep late. Tell Walt and Elmer all you do before breakfast is smooth your cot, and shine some things. No hogs to slop, feed to pitch, mash to mix, wood to split, fire to lay. Practically nothing.

Tell Walt and Elmer if they were here they would have to shave but it is not so bad, there's warm water. Breakfast is strong on trimmings like fruit juice, cereal, eggs, bacon, etc., but kind of weak on chops, potatoes, ham, steak, fried eggplant, pie and other regular food, but tell Walt and Elmer you can always sit by the two city boys that live on coffee. Their food plus yours holds you till noon when you get fed again.

It's no wonder these city boys can't walk much. We go on "route marches," which the platoon sergeant says are long walks to harden us. If he thinks so, it's not my place to tell him different. A "route march" is about as far as to our mailbox at home. Then the city guys get sore feet and we all ride back in trucks.

The country is nice but awful flat. The sergeant is like a school teacher. He nags a lot. The Captain is like the school board. Majors and colonels just ride around and frown. They don't bother you none.

This next will kill Walt and Elmer with laughing. I keep getting medals for shooting. I don't know why. The bulls-eye is near as

100

big as a chipmunk head and don't move, and it ain't shooting at you like the Higgett boys at home. All you got to do is lie there all comfortable and hit it. You don't even load your own cartridges. They come in boxes.

Then we have what they call hand-to-hand combat training. You get to wrestle with them city boys. I have to be real careful though, they break real easy. It ain't like fighting with that ole bull at home. I'm about the best they got in this except for that Tug Jordan from over in Silver Lake. I only beat him once. He joined up the same time as me, but I'm only 5'6" and 130 pounds and he's 6'8" and near 300 pounds dry.

Be sure to tell Walt and Elmer to hurry and join before other fellers get onto this setup and come stampeding in.

Your loving daughter,

Carol

Wow! Got you, didn't I? Didn't expect a girl, did you? It got me too the first time I read it. We usually don't think of women with terms like tough and strong. On behalf of all you women out there, I will now inform the rest of humanity – which leaves only the male species—women are tough! Women are not wimps!

According to the U.S. Department of Health and Human Services, the average woman in the U.S. is 5' 3.7" tall and weighs 152 pounds. Stop it! You are comparing yourself to the average, aren't you? The woman's average is certainly smaller than the average male. However, dynamite comes in small packages, and small doesn't mean weak. Don't see images of Demi Moore as G.I. Jane when you think of a woman's toughness. Neither should you limit your tough woman concept to the pioneer mountain woman. Grouchy Granny Clampett and her feisty niece Ellie Mae would be classified as tough for sure. The marine and mountain women aside, the rest of you women are tough, too. We men often think a woman's toughness can only be gauged in a "man's world." So the girls who wear football suits, engage in mud wrestling, work on a construction site, fight fires, wear a police uniform, or serve in the military are seen as the examples of women who are truly tough. While these certainly are demonstrating toughness, I suggest that the place to find out how tough women really are is in the labor and delivery room at your local hospital. At the delivery room, macho men have to step aside as Mama shows them what tough is all about.

God knew a man has his limitations, so he gave the hard work to women. Birthing a baby is not shift work. What kind of work would you call it? How do you describe the pain that must accompany the experience of pushing something the size of a basketball through something the size of a water hose? We'll stick with the Bible here—we'll call it a curse! A few generations ago, as an American you would have witnessed this toughness at the end of the row in a garden or a few yards away inside the little wooden shack in which she lived. Today in many third world countries, women are still birthing their babies in wilderness conditions without medical assistance. A trip to the mountains of Honduras, the plains of Africa, or the mountains of India quickly reveals the conditions that women live in and birth babies into. Think about having a baby within sight of an angry rhinoceros, cape buffalo, or hungry lion. This is not fiction but fact for many women in the world. In the best of conditions, it is labor intensive. In poverty stricken conditions, it is almost unthinkable.

I am amazed at the resilience, courage, and outright toughness that women demonstrate in order to keep the generations following one another. Having babies, now that's tough. Having babies without pain killers—now that's what we call here in the South being "tough as a pine knot."

I had the wonderful privilege of being present (live as it happened) in the delivery room for the birth of each of our children. This was when I discovered just how tough women are. In the early nineties, we lived in Senatobia, Mississippi, a small city about 45 miles south of Memphis, Tennessee. Mikki, my wife, was pregnant at the time with our third child. I still vividly recall the events of that brisk November morning in 1992. Mikki awakened me about 2:20 a.m. Her water had broken. Contractions had awakened her and stood her on her feet. When this happens with child number one—you panic! It unleashes a string of crazy behaviors in the husband that all link together to prove he is a lunatic.

-Run out the house in the middle of the night half naked.
-Squeal out the driveway.
-Go back and get the wife.
-Race down the interstate.
-Ask your wife a million questions even though she doesn't want to talk.
-Sweat bullets and pray in tongues even if you don't believe in it.
-Call on God to slow down what your wife has prayed for weeks for God to speed up.
-Run red lights and pass State Troopers.
-Slide in the parking lot leaving long black rubber streaks to mark the birth of your child.
-Run into the hospital screaming "Emergency!"
-Go back out and get the wife.

Since this was our third child, thankfully, both of us were calm and steady. We knew what to expect. We had time. I got up and took a quick shower, loaded up Andrew and Kara Beth (our two older children), and we were off. We stopped by a friend's house to leave the kids and continued our leisurely pre-dawn drive to Baptist East Memorial Hospital in Memphis, Tennessee. We planned about an hour on the road. Mikki's labor quickly started gaining speed and so did our Toyota. Things were now moving much faster than the previous two times we had been through the routine. I turned north onto I-55 and pressed the gas pedal on our little white Toyoto Tercel 4x4 station wagon to the floor. The motor was humming, the car was vibrating, and we were headed north to the land of Tennessee where our baby would be born.

About 35 minutes up the interstate, we neared the city of Southaven, Mississippi. The Baptist Hospital there was just off the interstate. Seeing the lights in the distance, Mikki informed me that we might ought to stop there. She was hurting, and the contractions were growing closer and closer

> **I said to her, "Hold on!" Let me tell you, that's a stupid thing to say to a woman who is having contractions about to birth a baby.**

together. I said to her, "Hold on!" Let me tell you, that's a stupid thing to say to a woman who is having contractions about to birth a baby. It's not like telling your four-year-old to hold it a little while longer. It's like throwing a bowling ball and a micro-second before you release the ball, trying to change your mind. Too late—something is going to happen, and it's probably going to hurt. From the way Mikki looked at me when I told her to "Hold on", I began to think I was going to get hurt. Anyway, I looked at my speedometer which was reading almost 100 MPH. Our little car was groaning and so was my little wife. I don't know what possessed me not to stop at the Mississippi hospital. I said, "This baby is not going to be born in Mississippi!" No offense to you Mississippians but for some reason, I didn't want my baby born in Mississippi, and we kept moving. I had Tennessee on my mind. That was where her doctor was. We knew him and felt comfortable with him. That was what we planned. So, as a man, I stuck to the plan.

In much less than the anticipated hour, we pulled into the parking lot of the hospital in Memphis. I stopped at the door, took her in, and then parked the car. By the time I filled out paperwork and made it to the room, the doctor and nurses were already working with Mikki. I was busy trying to load film into the video camera when the doctor informed me that I should put on my scrubs. "I'll do it in just a minute Doc!" I blurted out as I continued loading the camera. He said, "If you want to see this baby born, do it now!" My receiver finally tuned in, and I got the message. While I jumped into my little yellow scrubbies, I watched them hurriedly try to put a big long needle into Mikki's spine to deaden the pain. I am not exaggerating, that needle was terrifyingly long and seemed the size of a small drinking straw. I'm thinking, "This is what they stick in a woman's spine to keep it all from hurting!" Wow! Are women tough or what? The big long needle was just the pre-game show. They stuck her with the needle, but they never got to turn on the "feel good stuff." Time was up. No negotiating. The baby was heading out. It was our third child. This time I had gotten her to the hospital too late.

My precious little 5"-0" tall wife is a real W-O-M-A-N! I watched her deliver Elliott, our third born, without a word. She grimaced and clenched her teeth and birthed our baby naturally—pain and all. I thought they could have at the least put a wood stick or piece of leather in her mouth like they did on Gunsmoke. That always seemed to help Marshall Matt Dillon when they had to cut a bullet out of him. I remember thinking, this is one tough woman. Elliott was born at 5:20 a.m., a mere 40 minutes after we had arrived at the hospital. That's what you call, cutting it close. It was tough, but I want you to know, I made it through. Thank you for your concern.

Mikki really did amaze me. In just a little bit, she was on her feet and doing great. Don't let anyone tell you that women aren't tough! If *"How much pain can you take?"* is the question that determines toughness, then women carry home the trophy. I have passed kidney stones without medication. This was about as much fun as eating thumb tacks. I can only imagine what an 8 pound baby would be like. The prize for pain tolerance goes to the women. Give them the cake, the blue ribbon, the hat and the kazoo. We men are relegated to being the chauffeurs who carry them to the place of pain where a woman becomes a mother.

Compared to what a woman endures during this process (even with the wonder of modern medicine), men could be viewed as whiny, spineless wimps. Sorry guys! This is not to diminish your macho image or the brawny mental pictures you have on display in the gallery of your mind. However, we have to give women their due. God gave them quite a job to do in carrying within their bodies the hope of the next generation. God chose to have the woman carry the life of the children that would extend our own lives. They have been called, created, and anointed to do this. What a high calling! What a tremendous honor and responsibility. What a painful proposition.

This calling was in place before Adam and Eve's fall into sin. The Fall brought the pain, but the call to give birth was in God's original intentions. The woman was created to be like the man but different. She is the same as him in many ways but also different than him in many ways. The 1928 edition of Webster's Dictionary defines a "woman" as a man with a womb. Only the woman is able to carry the child that represents the next generation. Without her, the future is impossible, and man could not reproduce. Without her, we would be dreadfully incomplete, not to mention non-existent.

It is also interesting that it was the woman that the serpent chose to target. Was it because of her weakness or because of her strength? She was created to be the carrier of the first human being ever to be born from the womb of another human being? As I wrote about in my book,

> **Only the woman is able to carry the child that represents the next generation.**

Breath of God, the womb of woman is the place where God has chosen to continue His creative activity. He is the giver and source of life. In the womb of a woman, He is at work forming and fashioning human life -- the only life on the planet that bears His image. Though marred, humanity still carries the image of their awesome Creator. It was Eve who was chosen to carry the future. Inside Adam's body was the seed for the next generation. Inside Eve's body were the eggs and environment where the next generation would be conceived, grown, and developed. The truth of the matter is that the womb of a woman has always been the object of Satan's hatred. The womb symbolized humanity's destiny and Satan's demise all at the same time. Could this have been in Paul's mind in the very controversial passage we read in 1 Timothy 2:15?

1 Tim. 2:15 Nevertheless she will be saved in childbearing if they continue in faith, love, and holiness, with self-control.

> **The truth of the matter is that the womb of a woman has always been the object of Satan's hatred.**

Could it be that women have gotten a bad rap down through the centuries? Could it be that they have been exploited as frail, weak, and unlearned, when in fact God Himself designed her and decreed over her that she would be the means to deliver the One through Whom He would overthrow evil and the evil one? Every time a woman battles through the pain of giving birth, she is squaring off with the consequences of the curse. Who can question the courage and the strength seen in a woman protecting her children? Church history is replete with the advances made in the spirit by faithful women. Most local churches see their work advanced because of faithful women. Thank God for His faithful daughters. The woman is the weaker vessel according to 1 Peter 3:7. This does not mean inferior, and it does not mean spiritually weaker. It does not mean she is without strength. In the spirit, which is the most important, she is man's equal. She is strong, but she is a lady.

A Lady?
Yes!
But a Lady Warrior!

Chapter Nine
The Restoration of All Things

If you read history you will find that the Christians who did most for the present world were precisely those who thought most of the next. It is since Christians have largely ceased to think of the other world that they have become so ineffective in this. - C. S. Lewis

~

While this book deals with what the Bible says about women, it does not probe into all the controversial passages that have been used for centuries to keep women silent. As I mentioned earlier, there are some excellent works that shed light on these Scriptures such as Loren Cunningham and David Joel Hamilton's book, *Why Not Women?*[17] However, I do want to give you something to think about concerning the idea of restoration.

When putting together a puzzle, it helps to see the picture on the box in order to get a better glimpse of how the pieces snap together. Without the picture on the box, it just takes longer. If we can see God's original intentions for man and woman in Eden before sin entered the human race, it will help us to know where God is heading as He restores things. Eden is our picture on the front of the box. Knowing what God is putting back together through the redemptive power of the cross of Jesus Christ will hopefully help speed up the process. The Bible tells us that God is going to restore all things before everything is summed up here on earth. I remind you that the religious leaders of Jesus' day thought they knew what the coming of the Messiah would be

> Eden is our picture on the front of the box.

like, but they were not seeing the picture on the box clearly. He stood before them, yet they did not see Him as the Messiah. Paul teaches us in 1 Corinthians 13:12 that we prophesy in part and that we see through a glass darkly. One day the perfect will arrive—the Second Coming of Jesus and the restoration of all things. This is when things will become completed. The truth of the matter is that none of us see all the prophecies absolutely clearly. None of us have all the pieces of the puzzle figured out. The last question Jesus' disciples asked Him before He ascended had to do with a piece of the prophetic puzzle—*"Will the kingdom be restored to Israel at this time?"* (Matthew 17:11, Acts 1:6-7). They were trying to put it all together. Jesus told them that His Father was the only One who could answer the time question but that they should get busy witnessing to the world through the power of the Holy Spirit (Acts 1). Good advice for us, too!

When we put a puzzle together, we usually start with the border pieces that form the frame around the edge—correct? My friend, Floyd Spivey, shared with me that this represents the boundaries. He is right! That's where we usually start, right? The boundaries represent the outer parameters. Where are the parameters of what God is going to do in these last days? There is an intriguing passage of Scripture found in Acts 3 that sums up the divine plan of God. It is very relevant to us today. The passage tells us what God is in the process of doing. It gives us a glimpse of the picture on the box and tells us how God has the past in mind as He moves us into our future. He is restoring so He can complete His original purpose among humankind.

Acts 3:19 Repent therefore and be converted, that your sins may be blotted out, so that times of refreshing may come from the presence of the Lord, 20 and that He may send Jesus Christ, who was preached to you before, 21 whom heaven must receive until the times of restoration of all things, which God has spoken by the mouth of all His holy prophets since the world began.

Note the sequence in this passage:

• Repentance
• Conversion
• Blotting out of Sins
• Appointed Times of Refreshing from God's Presence
• Process of Restoration of All Things
• Fulfillment of All Prophecies Spoken
• Return of Jesus Christ from Heaven

Each of these is worthy of a separate chapter but to stay on track for the subject at hand, I call your attention to the phrases "restoration of all things" and "since the world began."

The term "restoration" or as the KJV states it "restitution" is a powerful word. Albert Barnes in his commentary says, "The noun rendered restitution (*apokatastaseoos)* does not elsewhere occur in the New Testament. The verb from which it is derived occurs eight times. It means properly "to restore a thing to its former situation," as restoring a "strained" or "dislocated" limb to its former soundness. Hence, it is used to restore, or to heal, in the New Testament:[18]

The second phrase, "since the world began", needs no clarification. It tells us the boundaries of the prophetic puzzle. All the prophecies beginning with the one God Himself decreed in the Garden of Eden after Adam and Eve sinned state that God is working to bring things back to the way they were before sin entered the human race. When restoration is used it is in reference to putting something back the way it was at some time before. The passage tells us the standard—the way it was when the world began. Sin created a parenthesis in the history of humanity. We are still in the parenthesis. The birth, ministry, death, burial, and resurrection are the centerpiece of restoration. Jesus came to atone for sin, destroy the works of the Devil, bring humanity back into relationship with God, and extend the kingdom of God throughout the world.

Matt 24:14 And this gospel of the kingdom will be preached in all the world as a witness to all the nations, and then the end will come.

When this is done, and all is ready, then He will return and God's original purposes will be carried out for all eternity. God is always raising up forerunners to usher in the changes that bring restoration. I cover this in more detail in my book, *The Forerunner Anointing: Preparing for the Restoration of All Things*[19]. There is no denying from the Acts 3 passage that Peter recognized that certain things had to happen before Jesus returned and those things related to the restoration of God's original purposes.

This has a very specific bearing on women and their role in the end times. If God is bringing about the restoration of all things, then what was woman like prior to the entrance of sin? What consequences did she suffer as a result of her sin? These questions enable us to see what should be undone in order for all things to be restored. Also, it is important to realize that there are other areas where this same principle has clearly demonstrated

> **If God is bringing about the restoration of all things, then what was woman like prior to the entrance of sin?**

itself in the body of Christ. For example, Paul wrote to slaves to be good slaves. He wrote to slave masters to be good slave masters, but he never addressed the wrongness of slavery. Why? Did he not realize it was wrong?

Living in the first century was a completely different experience than living in the twenty-first century. Slavery was rampant. It was an accepted practice during the Old Testament culture and carried into the New Testament culture. It obviously was not God's time to deal with it. However, the body of Christ has dealt with it. It would be unthinkable for a church today to write into its constitution and bylaws how members who are slaves should be treated. This is now a past issue, at least for a great part of the world. Slavery still exists, but it has been greatly reduced and is globally unacceptable. It takes time for some truth to work itself into culture. The book of Hebrews is a standing reminder to us that the early Jewish believers had a battle transitioning from offering their sacrifices at the temple to resting in the finished sacrifice of Christ. It took a while for it all to make sense. Most of the letters written to the early churches by the Apostles had to deal with clearing up doctrinal and functional issues. When it comes to the issue of women in the church and in society, the same applies. For centuries, women were denied the privileges of men. Even the temple made according to the pattern prescribed by God did not allow the women past the outer area. We must remember that the Old Testament was based on the law of God. The law was a schoolmaster that showed us our sin and brought us to Christ to be rescued. Sin placed humankind under a curse, and Jesus came to become a curse for us to deliver us from its power. If part of the consequence of sin was that it caused women to be ruled over by men, then should we not expect to see God moving to break its power in this area? Should we not see a change in men's attitudes toward women? There should be the restoration of honor, respect, and value that Adam gave Eve before the Fall and Jesus gave women when He walked the earth. Paul reminds us in Ephesians 5:25 that the way a husband is to love his wife is modeled in the way Christ loves His bride, the church. He gave His life for her. Instead of trampling on her, He laid down His life for her.

It is clear that Adam listened to Eve, and she spoke into his life before the Fall of humanity into sin. This is the very area the enemy targeted. He cleverly devised a scheme to shut down the woman's voice. Shouldn't we see God moving in history to restore her voice?

In the early church, it is apparent that women began stepping into uncharted waters by speaking publicly, praying publicly, and prophesying publicly. They may not have always used these opportunities wisely but it is clear they had the opportunities. Could it be that some of the corrective passages were written to deal with local situations that got out of hand? If not, then we must

117

conclude that God never intended for women to have their voice restored. If this is true, then what does that say about the power of the blood of Jesus to restore? Was it a work of the devil that got Eve into trouble to start with? Did Jesus die to destroy that work, too? If it is destroyed, then shouldn't woman's voice be trustworthy again?

Acts 3 passage states that all things that the prophets have prophesied will be fulfilled. Those who are saved will ultimately be in a place where there is no sin, like it was in the Garden. At the end of the Book of The Revelation, God's children will see His face, live by His river, and eat from fruit that is borne by two trees of life. There will be no curse, no sin, no sorrow and no pain (Rev. 22:1-5). This certainly seems like an Eden upgrade.

Because all the prophecies foretold since the world began will be fulfilled, we can see glimpses of the future by looking at them. Are there prophecies about women that were foretold? Yes! Of special note to women is a prophecy from the Old Testament Prophet Joel. This was the passage that Peter used to announce the outpouring of the Spirit on the day of Pentecost.

Acts 2:16 But this is what was spoken by the prophet Joel: 17'And it shall come to pass in the last days, says God, That I will pour out of My Spirit on all flesh; Your sons and your daughters shall prophesy, your young men shall

see visions, your old men shall dream dreams. **18 And on My menservants and on My maidservants I will pour out My Spirit in those days; And they shall prophesy. 19 I will show wonders in heaven above and signs in the earth beneath: Blood and fire and vapor of smoke. 20 The sun shall be turned into darkness, and the moon into blood, Before the coming of the great and awesome day of the LORD. 21 And it shall come to pass that whoever calls on the name of the LORD shall be saved.'**

Notice some of the highlights of the passage:

- Pentecost inaugurated the time-frame of history called the "last days."
- It will come to pass.
- The Holy Spirit will be poured out.
- There will be no discrimination concerning who can receive the Holy Spirit. It will be for all flesh.
- Sons and daughters will have revelatory experiences and will share those experiences with others (visions and prophesying).
- Old men will have revelatory experiences (dreams).
- Even men and women slaves will prophesy.
- There will be cosmic signs and wonders in the heavens prior to Jesus' return to Earth.
- The Day of the Lord will come, and it will be clearly visible and evident when it does.
- Salvation will be available for those who ask.

This is such an awesome passage. Can you imagine its power spoken over people with a first century context concerning women? The idea of women having the Holy Spirit poured out upon them and daughters and maidservants prophesying was

Our God is a God of restoration.

radical. They were used to seeing the anointing oil poured on the heads of men, now they witnessed tongues of fire resting on the heads of women. They were being told the Spirit was being poured out on women. Notice also that the Joel passage Peter uses says these things will happen "Before the coming of the great and awesome day of the LORD." Then in the next chapter on the next occasion that Peter preaches, he shares the passage about restoration of all things that have been prophesied before Jesus returns. It is clear from a New Testament perspective, that the day of Pentecost marked a transition point for women in the kingdom of God. It is taking awhile for it all to take root, but it will before Jesus returns on the great and awesome Day of the LORD. This day of Second Coming glory is closer now than it has ever been, therefore look for God to release and raise up the voice of women as never before. The Lord will have His way as Isaiah reminds us:

Isa 46:9 Remember the former things of old,
For I am God, and there is no other;
I am God, and there is none like Me,

**10 Declaring the end from the beginning,
And from ancient times things that are not yet done,
Saying,'My counsel shall stand,
And I will do all My pleasure,'**

Our God is a God of restoration. He sees the end from the
beginning and knows how it is all supposed to fit together.
He has declared things from ancient times that are not yet
done. What He has spoken will stand. He will do what
pleases Him. Expect to see the restoration of all things that
have been prophesied since the world began. There is no
opposing power in the universe that can keep God's
decreed Word from coming to pass. What God says is
powerful. Unfortunately there are a lot of women who have
not yet heard about God's plans for them.

Chapter Ten
The Big Announcement

Remember, Ginger Rogers did everything Fred Astaire did, but backwards and in high heels. –Faith Whittlesey

~

Deep in the spiritual DNA of every woman, I believe there is a distant memory of a time when woman was a princess beside her prince. She was a queen beside her king. She was in perfect union with her husband, and together they were partners walking in the realm of Earth with the power and authority of heaven. She was unfettered by the man's desire to make her the object of his dominion. She was not held back, abused or belittled. She too had dominion, and she and her man were the original dynamic duo. I believe the heart of God is to restore things back to their original order and intention. This is what the story of the cross is all about. Through the power of the cross, the bad stuff is turned around, and women can once again began to take their proper place in God's kingdom here on the earth. Her pre-sin position was one of mutual power and dominion along side her husband. She knew who she was and she knew what she had. Every woman should know what God says she has and who God says she is.

On a special September Saturday night in Atlantic City, New Jersey, a beautiful ballroom fit for a princess had been prepared. The air was filled with energy and excitement. An opinionated audience sat waiting to hear the announcement of the name of the 1995 Miss America. Five beautiful young women were on stage holding their breath in anticipation of possibly hearing their own name. In living rooms across America and around the world, an anxious audience awaited the announcement. Bragging rights were narrowed down to the five states of Georgia, Alabama, New Jersey, Virginia, and Indiana. The Master of Ceremonies, Regis Philbin, began opening the envelopes announcing the second runner-up and first runner-up. Then, with pause and power, he made the grand announcement to the ears of a waiting world. The audience in the auditorium, the viewing audience across America and around the world, and everyone on the platform heard the name of the 1995 Miss America announced. Everyone, that is, except the young woman who won. Heather Whitestone from Alabama was named Miss America. The beautiful and talented young lady from Alabama was deaf and unable to audibly hear Philbin's announcement. Though everyone else knew, it was a few moments before she realized she was Miss America. Finally, the contestant standing at her side informed her that she had won. Once she understood that she was Miss America, her heart flooded with that "dream come true" kind of joy. Heather and all America along with her rejoiced at what she had accomplished.[20] It

124

was a night to remember. Women around the world, like Heather, are still waiting to hear the truth about the position of honor that they have been given. They have not heard God's big announcement of their true identity and destiny. Once they do, it will change their lives. It will energize them with purpose and confidence by knowing that God Himself ordained them to be women filled with power and purpose.

It could be that you are one of Daddy God's girls who has not yet heard and understood who you really are. I want to share with you a "Big Announcement" that God

Women—you are not an afterthought of God!

made in the garden that may have never reached your ears. Many are beginning to hear about it, now it's time for you to hear. Women—you are not an afterthought of God! You were on God's mind before Adam was ever formed. When God formed Adam out of the dust of the ground, He knew He would be making a woman from one of the ribs in Adam's side. God had something very special in mind when He created woman. In the first two chapters of Genesis, the Bible records seven times when God looked at what He had created and said it was good. Only once did He declare that something was not good. The only time God said something was not good is when Man existed on the earth without woman. God declared that it was not good for man to be alone.[21] Father God never intended a world without women. In order for man to do what God had created him to do, there had to be a woman. And in order for woman to do what God had created her to do, there had to be a man. As a result of this, God caused a deep sleep to fall upon Adam. While Adam slept, God reached into his side, pulled out a rib, and made a woman.

My wife, Mikki, and I have a short list of favorite romantic movies. Near the top of the list is the 1995 romantic comedy, *While You Were Sleeping*.[22] We love to watch Lucy, Sandra Bullock's character, as her dream comes true—but in a way much differently than she had expected. Our hearts always flutter at the end of the movie when her new found love, Jack, drops the engagement ring into the tray where she sits receiving tokens from passengers boarding the Chicago Transit. The plot of the movie revolves around a man in a coma and the twisted and tangled circumstances that Lucy was pulled into as a result of saving her dream man's life… the dream man who does not know she exists.

Then suddenly everyone thinks she is Peter's (the unconscious man's) fiancé. In the middle of the mayhem, Lucy falls in love with Peter's brother, Jack. It was love at second sight. Lucy discovers that *who* she is and *what* she wanted was different than she had thought. Life surprises us as we discover the truth about ourselves. The movie ends with Lucy narrating how it all turned out. She said, "Peter once asked me when it was that I fell in love with Jack. And I told him, it was while you were sleeping." It's a story with an ending that calls for the tissue.

A lot happened while Adam was sleeping, too. He awakened to meet the love of his life. She came from Adam, but she was not made by Adam. She was created by God. Before Eve ever met Adam, she met God. She saw God before she saw Adam. Before she ever felt the touch of Adam's hand upon her life, she felt the touch of God's hand upon her life. She was not Adam's idea, she was God's idea. When Eve was brought to Adam, he welcomed her into his life. He received her as an expression and extension of himself. Theirs was a perfect marriage. They were both naked and unashamed. Some time later, we do not know just how long, the bad stuff started. A bad choice was made, and the communication between the two was directly damaged. From the day that Eve ate of the tree and gave to her husband to eat, women have had a tough time. They live in a world different from the world that was left in Eden. Why is it that it seems that men and women have difficulty understanding and relating to one another? I have an idea about that. It also is found in Genesis three.

Chapter Eleven
Why Men Don't Listen
When Women Speak!

Women like silent men. They think they're listening.
–Marcel Achard

~

Many men have hearing impairment. They have been stricken with female deafness. They don't hear a woman when she talks. I recently read a funny story that illustrates what I want to say in this chapter. It underscores the point that men are often too proud to admit their own failures and listen to what their wives have to say.

A concerned husband went to a doctor to talk about his wife. He says to the doctor, "Doctor, I think my wife is deaf because she never hears me the first time and always asks me to repeat things." "Well," the doctor replied, "go home and tonight stand about fifteen feet from her and say something to her. If she doesn't reply, move about five feet closer and say it again. Keep doing this so that we'll get an idea about the severity of her deafness."

Sure enough, the husband goes home and does exactly as instructed. He starts off about fifteen feet from his wife in the kitchen as she is chopping some vegetables and says, "Honey, what's for dinner?" He hears no response. He moves about five feet closer and asks again. No reply. He moves five feet closer. Still no reply. He gets fed up and moves right behind her, about an inch away, and asks again, "Honey, what's for dinner?" She replies, "For the fourth time, vegetable stew!" [23]

The truth is that Adam himself was barbed for listening to his wife and all we husbands since that time have arrived here with a wall up when it comes to a woman offering us advice. We only hear what we want to hear. When she whispers sweet nothings, we move closer and say "Speak on, sweetheart." However, when she brings up any other subject, we change channels and move away. We men have a problem receiving from the other half of the human race. We want their love but not their advice or counsel. God Himself spoke to Adam about his blunder.

Genesis 3:17 Then to Adam He said, "Because you have heeded the voice of your wife, and have eaten from the tree of which I commanded you, saying, 'You shall not eat of it':
"Cursed is the ground for your sake;
In toil you shall eat of it
All the days of your life.
18 Both thorns and thistles it shall bring forth for you,
And you shall eat the herb of the field.
19 In the sweat of your face you shall eat bread
Till you return to the ground,
For out of it you were taken;
For dust you are, And to dust you shall return."

"Because you have heeded the voice of your wife…." What stinging words—words that became engraved into Adam's subconscious mind. Don't you imagine that from that moment forward, Adam had an embedded resistance to heeding his wife's voice? It has been passed down to the rest of us hard-headed men. As the days following Eden unfolded and Adam was introduced to work that made him sweat, he thought of his mistake over and over and over. Why did I listen to her? What was I thinking? Because of this men carry a propensity to tune out the voice of women. Also I remind you that part of what Eve was told was that men would begin to have a desire to rule over women (Genesis 3:16). So as a result of sin, we guys also have within us a wrong desire to dominate women. This one-two punch has created quite a mess in the communication battles that exist between the sexes.

Let me be bold—Men also have another problem. We are proud! We do not like being told what to do—especially by a woman. Our ego reacts at the thought of being given directives by a woman. I suppose it is a hidden fear that we will be branded henpecked or sissy whipped. For me it is probably those unhealed memories of my sister beating me up when I was a preteen. She was four years older, bigger, and stronger than me at that time. I would start a fight with her, and she would finish it. We would fight, and she would win. Do you know what that does to a little mini-man? Whew! Pray for me. However, after I hit the teen years, I learned how to fight which turned things around. Then I got in trouble for beating up my sister—after which my Mama quickly corrected me with a proper spanking. Don't worry, I'm healed now—but I still have my moments.

My fingers tremble as I type because of the embarrassment that is forthcoming for me. Nevertheless, I have to admit that I have been guilty of the sin of being too proud to stop and ask for directions. I remember one occasion many years ago when we lived in Mississippi that we were traveling to a fried catfish place we had heard about at Bullfrog Corner. Yes, it's true—Bullfrog Corner! We had been given some simple

> **A man hates the suggestion that he stop and ask directions!**

directions to find the place. Isn't it amazing how one wrong turn can completely mess up a good set of directions? I did not know it at the time, but I was heading due east after a turn that should have been made to the west. I was driving the speed limit plus what grace allowed as I dreamed of the wonderful fried catfish that awaited me. I also was craving the chocolate-filled fried pies that others had so joyfully boasted of woofing down. Little did I know that I was racing away from the destination my stomach craved. I continued to mentally prepare for a luxurious southern dining experience. My head was absolutely at peace in the unknown lostness that I was racing into. Finally, my wife, Mikki, suggested that I had made a wrong turn. *"We should have been there by now!"* she bravely exclaimed. How dare she question my awareness of direction. After all, I grew up in the woods. Being geographically lost was not even in my vocabulary. My built-in compass had gotten me out of many a fix in the big woods. Becoming lost on the big wide open road was unthinkable. Unphased by my relentless pursuit of the famous fried catfish place, Mikki spoke up once again, *"Why don't you stop and ask someone for directions?"* Now I was really insulted. Dear lady reader, if no other sentence in this book were to fall upon the fertile soil of your believing heart, please allow the following one to find a resting place there.

A man hates the suggestion that he stop and ask directions! It is a barb into the deepest recesses of his prideful soul. It implies that he does not know where he is. He may be a macho man with a pioneer spirit but to imply he must ask for directions breaks him into little bitty microscopic pieces that the post-Fall Humpty Dumpty could hide in one of his little shirt pockets. As I sat pridefully perched behind the steering wheel of our car, I informed her once again that she should leave the navigation decisions to me. I continued my eastward trek toward the greasy object of my dining desires, unaware that I should have been traveling the westward route. Finally, a small leak of doubt began to spring into my stubborn mind. It did seem as if we had been traveling a long time to a place that was supposed to have been just a short distance off the interstate. Here's the pinch: if I was going the wrong way-a thought I was beginning to entertain-then there must be a reason other than the failure of my sharpened navigational abilities.

Maybe I had been given wrong directions.

If I had made a wrong turn, then it was probably while Mikki was talking and I had become distracted.

They could have moved the restaurant, and our friends did not know about it.

The last option was, "I had goofed."

All of a sudden, I thought of a great idea. Since I now needed to go to the restroom, I would pull off at the next service station. And since I had to do that, I could ask someone there about the location of the fried catfish place. As always my great idea worked, and we were told to turn around and go back where we had just come from and go across the interstate where we would see the restaurant just a short distance from the interstate. I had goofed. I found it hard to admit that my wife had been right. Somehow it had to be her fault, right? If I listened to her earlier, it would have saved us about 30 minutes of road time, and I could have had my fill of fried catfish and fried chocolate pie much sooner. There it is. I confessed my atrocious sin of stubbornness and pride. I resisted hearing what my wife tried to tell me. Fortunately, it was corrected, and we had a good time together. Yet, everyday men and their wives go through this scenario with results that are far more devastating than our little fried fish fiasco.

Women have to deal with this more than we men like to admit.

He never listens to me!
It doesn't matter what I say!
I tried to tell him, but it did no good.
He wants to know how his buddies feel about a situation but never cares how I feel.
The last time I warned him, he never admitted I was right.
He remembers his "I told you so moments" and always forgets mine!
I might as well be talking to a fencepost!
He turns the volume up on the TV when I try to share with him.
He is a clam.
He never shares.
H is note interested in what I have to share.

Many wives have had to struggle with feelings and thoughts such as these. Why is it that men often seem to ignore the counsel of their wives? Why is it that a woman's words seem to carry so little weight with men? Even when the woman is more experienced, has more personal knowledge of a situation and is better qualified to speak on a matter, she is often overlooked in a group of men when she offers her verbal contribution. I don't mean to make a blanket statement that reflects how all men and women feel on this matter. Yet, the truth is, there is some truth to these sentiments.

Some well-known and oft-quoted authors have braved to tell how they really feel about the role of women through their inflamed and frustrated pens. The following quote by George Bernard Shaw illustrates this frustration.

"Women upset everything. When you let them into your life, you find that the woman is driving at one thing and you're driving at another." [24]

Are women always driving at one thing and men another? Where is the place of unity? Yes, men and women are of the opposite sex, but does that mean they have to always be on the opposite side of the issues? Does it mean that men are to unilaterally govern the universe?

If that picture is too big, then does it mean that a man's own wife is not to have a place to speak into his life to help bring clarity and purpose whenever issues are being discussed? When did this friction first heat up between the sexes? Where did this happen? Has it always been this way?

Sometimes pushing the rewind button helps us uncover some clues as to why things are the way they are. Is this helpful? It can be, if you are seeking truth to help change things for the better. Can it be hurtful? Yes it can be, if it is a man on a mission seeking ammunition to win his debate and support his unwavering low regard for the place of a woman's voice.

If you are a woman who is frustrated with never being heard by your husband, it can be profitable to understand why he reacts the way he does. I think the answer to the root issue is found in the book of beginnings, Genesis. The occasion when the first married couple had their first falling out supplies us with some insight to where it all started.

Ladies, your great-great-great- great- ....grandmother, Eve and my great-great-great-great... grandfather Adam had their first encounter with evil as a result of Adam listening to Eve and Eve listening to the serpent. The deductive result-- men think the woman is easily deceived and speaks on behalf

> **Adam was individually responsible for what he did. He sinned with his eyes open.**

of the serpent. Truthfully, Adam was individually responsible for what he did. He sinned with his eyes open. He took and ate of the fruit simply because it was offered to him. However, I think that from that moment onward, Adam was especially cautious in allowing Eve to suggest where they would eat dinner. I also think that Eve became extremely cautious of offering advice to her husband on any issue. In simple terms, they both became gun shy because they had taken a big hit.

What does that have to do with us today? I believe that men and women carry an inherent woundedness rooted in the Fall. It has been passed on from father to son and mother to daughter down through the generations and is deeply rooted in our subconscious. There is a long- buried, distant memory of the serpent whispering in Eve's ear influencing her to speak his lies out of her mouth. We must be healed from this.

Farfetched?
Then what is your explanation?

Not concerning why your husband may have issues with listening to you, but why have men for centuries demonstrated this low regard for a woman's words and wisdom? Questions, questions, questions! I know, but the questions are an important part of the process of discovering the problem so that the solution can be applied.
It is my contention that since the Fall when Adam listened to Eve and disaster struck, that men have resisted the decision making ability of women. We tend to exclude them from our circles of decision makers. Deep inside the DNA is a distant distrust, an unhealed hurt. Part of the consequence announced by God is that men would begin to have the desire to rule over women. This desire to dominate has

choked out and suffocated the voices of many women. They are the unheard majority filled with giftedness and wisdom but excluded by our male mentalities. As Christian men who desire to follow Christ, we must remember that He listens to His bride. If prayer means anything—it means Jesus listens to His bride. Allow me to quote from my book, *Breath of God* to further illustrate this truth.

Marriage is a picture of Christ and His church. Husbands, you need to realize that Christ listens to His bride. He lives to make intercession for her. He does not ignore her. He gives Himself to her. There are times when Father wants to speak to us through our wives… I am reminded of an incident that happened a few years ago in which God used my wife to speak to me. This occurred on a Wednesday night at the conclusion of a service in which I had just preached. We had eaten a meal together, and it was followed by a worship service in the fellowship hall. At the conclusion of the service, one of the sweet little ladies of the church approached me. She said, "Brother Eddie, that message was so wonderful. The whole time that you were preaching, I saw a halo over your head." She went on and on about seeing the halo. In a few moments, she had me feeling like quite the angel. I thought, "Yea, a halo! Wow! Was I anointed or what?"

I strutted home to the parsonage where we lived at the time. I entered the house waltzing in glory thinking about how the Lord had given visual evidence of my preaching prowess. What an anointing must have fallen upon me. It must have been reminiscent of the transfiguration of Jesus. Mikki who had arrived home earlier, walked down the hall toward me. I was preparing to tell her about this great manifestation of glory that had fallen upon me while I had been preaching. I thought she might not have noticed it. Before I could address her, she stopped, and blurted out, "You need to get someone to adjust the spotlights in the fellowship hall. The whole time you were preaching tonight, they were glaring off your bald head." Oh! What a dagger to the heart! I tried to accuse her of not being nearly as spiritual as the little lady at the church. As I said, sometimes the Lord speaks to husbands through their wives. They often carry the punch that needs to be delivered to our pride to keep us humble…

Adam and Eve, the perfect son and his perfect wife, ultimately failed Father. God had a plan to redeem His fallen children. Jesus, the last Adam, came and laid down His life in the sleep of death, so that His Father could take from His side what was needed to make a wife suitable for Him. The bride of Christ comes to the Father through the Son. When this happens, God begins the work of making her all she needs to be in order to present her back to His Son. There will come a day when she will be presented to Jesus, and she will have no spots, blemishes, wrinkles, or any such thing (Eph 5:27). She came from His side, and she will stand as bride at His side. God has ordained that we, as the bride of Christ, are to be one with Him. [25]

It is clear to see that Jesus models for us a sacrificial love that cherishes and respects the input and voice of His bride.

We must allow the grace of God to help us embrace His original intentions so that men and women can be who God created them to be. Before their fall into sin, Adam had fully embraced and welcomed Eve into his life. There was no distrust or suspicion. Jesus died to restore us to the same place.

Chapter Twelve
What a Man's Voice Does to a Woman

Being a woman is a terribly difficult task, since it consists principally in dealing with men. –Joseph Conrad

~

I believe one of the keys to the restoration of the voice of women is the release of the voice of men. When men begin decreeing the right things, it will open the way for the voice of women to be heard. Do the biological math. There are only the voices of men and women among humanity. If women's voices are not being heard, it is because men's ears are not listening. This means that men listen to men. Therefore, if men would release within the hearing of other men the truth of restoration, then men would begin honoring and receiving from the voice of women. We must pray for courageous men to arise and release the message of the restoration of women.

We must tear down the fears concerning the voice of women. Some men fear the voice of seduction. Yes, there are women who seduce—they use the influence of their voice to lure a man into sin. The book of Proverbs contains such warnings for us. Yet, to think that all voices of women are voices of seduction is absurd. Men are able to seduce with their words as well. Since all humanity fell into sin, then all our voices came under the sway of the curse and have to be restored, right? The simple truth is that we all, men and women, fell into sin together, and God is bringing us out together.

The first occasion a human being ever spoke to another human being happened when Adam spoke to the woman God brought to him. The words he spoke were in essence words of equality—*"You're like me!"*

Genesis 2:23 And Adam said:
"This is now bone of my bones
And flesh of my flesh;
She shall be called Woman,
Because she was taken out of Man."

These first words also contained the truth that became the focus of Satan's first attack against them. The devil knew if he could create conflict between the sexes, he could create chaos in the whole culture and possibly thwart the purposes of God. God Himself later informed the first couple that there would be an issue between them that would result in men ruling over women. But remember, they were originally intended to rule together.

 When you look at this sequence of events in the creation of man and woman, you should notice the power of the man's words spoken into the life of the woman. When Adam first saw Eve, his response was a verbal affirming powerful decree—*you are bone of my bones, flesh of my flesh!* It was an affirmation of acceptance. The woman knew from the man's first words that he was pleased with her—he liked her—he was excited by her—he was thrilled to meet her and to step into the future with her. Adam decreed over his wife that they were one because she came from him. This is important to note in the divine order. The first words a human being ever heard from another human being were words of acceptance and

> **The first words a human being ever heard from another human being were words of acceptance and unity.**

unity. To paraphrase the import of what Adam said, it is like he was saying, *"Wow! You're like me. You came from me. We are in this together."*

These powerful words all occurred before sin entered the human race. It was after sin entered that Adam first spoke words that accused, embarrassed, and exposed his wife. He said accusingly to God, *"The woman you gave me gave me the fruit and I ate."* The previous chapter goes into some detail about this; however, I want to take you down another trail concerning this breech of communication that occurred between the sexes. Because the serpent worked through the woman speaking to the man to try to reverse God's plans, now Father is working through men to release affirming decrees as part of the process of restoring women.

How unfortunate it is when a man looses his voice against a woman in a condemning, condescending way. A man's voice used in this way has the same effect that the serpent's voice did in the Garden—guilt and condemnation. We, as men, must rise up in the opposite spirit of the serpent and in the same spirit as Father and decree the value and victory of women. We must allow the Holy Spirit through the blood of Jesus to cover the image of the fallen Eve in our minds and replace it with the image of the women at the tomb who arose from clinging to Jesus feet to go spread the good news that Christ is risen! When this happens, we are reflecting that we are sons of the last Adam who is restoring what was lost by the first Adam.

Adam voiced acceptance and affirmation of Eve before sin entered the Garden of Eden, so as the sons of the last Adam, we must lift our voices and embrace the restoration of the voice of women. Step back into Genesis three with me for another moment. Adam pointed his finger at his bride and basically said—*"She did it!"* Men have been blaming women ever since. It is true that she gave the fruit to Adam. It was true she was first deceived. It is also true that he took it. It is true that he also knew better. It is also true that he did not step between the serpent and his bride like Daddy God later did. When Jesus came, He did step between His bride and all the sting and pain of sin and death. What did He do? He took it all upon Himself. Why? To cover His bride so she would be free and clean. I wonder what might have happened had the first Adam not eaten of the fruit and had offered himself to Father in behalf of his bride in order to cover her and redeem her? Just a thought, but it is what Jesus, the last Adam, did do.

What Adam did not do, Father did. He addressed the serpent. He decreed that the serpent would be crushed and the woman would be saved and rescued by the Deliverer. It is through child bearing that all women and the rest of us have ultimately been able to be redeemed. When Jesus came, He strapped on His war boots and stomped the evil out of our futures! Praise His Name! I have already written about how Father's words must have lifted Eve's spirit and filled her heart with hope. Think about the impact of His words on her. Could it be that all women carry them the memory of Father's words spoken over Eve? Could it be that there is also a distant feeling of fear associated with the first words of accusation that Adam spoke over her?

Women need the verbal affirmation and acceptance of men in their lives. This is part of what they were given in the Garden before sin, and it is needed now in the restoration from sin. I do not say this to indicate weakness, but as a desire for completeness. When my wife read the previous chapter, she commented to me that it caused her to understand why it meant so much to her when I voice approval and acceptance to her. She said it made her feel loved and protected. I believe in marriage that the husband is to provide spiritual covering for his wife. The first woman opened her eyes under the covering of her Father (God). He carried her to the man who would become her husband (Adam). The Bible declares that a man would leave his father and mother and be joined to his wife. As a result, they become one (Gen. 2:24). In the sexual relationship, when a man covers a woman the possibility of fruitfulness occurs. In the womb of the woman, the life of their offspring grows and is protected and nourished. She is very vulnerable during this time. When the baby arrives, she gives her attention to nurturing the little one. The husband/father provides and protects and covers them both. This is the way God intended family to operate.

Part of the way a husband covers his wife is through the words he speaks over her. A man's words are powerful when spoken into the life of his wife. I challenge all you men who may read this book to speak words of life into the life of your wife. Tell her you love her. Voice your approval and acceptance. Bless her place and role as a woman. Eliminate any accusing or condemning words. Allow God to use your voice to restore the power of her voice. As Adam did before sin, communicate with her that she is one with you—bone of your bones, flesh of your flesh. Before God brought the woman to

> **When we have unhealed wounds near our heart, we release words that compare our spouse to the people who have hurt us.**

the man in the Garden, He closed up Adam's side. Allow God to heal you as well. It is important that the wounds of our past be healed so that we will release words that affirm instead of words that condemn. When we have unhealed wounds near our heart, we release words that compare our spouse to the people who have hurt us. We speak out of our hurt instead out of our healing. Our words reproduce after their own kind.

In the body of Christ, it is important that men voice acceptance of the woman's voice and allow the woman's voice to be heard. It is not a competition—it is a team. Remember, we must think of the original intentions of Father toward women, not what man has made it to be. It is a minority of women who are calling for the overthrow of the voice of men. The majority simply want the blessing and acceptance of men given to them to be who God has

> **Most women are not warring to be the head over man—they are warring to stand at his side and work with him.**

called them to be—mighty women of God standing at the side of men doing the work of the kingdom together out of their equal position in Christ. For too long men have felt called to be the gatekeepers who keep women in her place. The problem is that we have had them in the wrong place. We are called to be the gatekeepers to war against the curse of sin and open the gates for the restoration of women in culture. Most women are not warring to be the head over man—they are warring to stand at his side and work with him. For too long they have been made to kneel at his feet instead of the feet of Jesus. In the church, we are all positionally the bride of Christ.

We men must also open our eyes and see what God is doing in this hour among women. It is undeniable that God is using the voices of women globally to advance the kingdom. All around us, women are arising in dominion and authority walking out their God given destinies. Consider Aglow International as an example of the influence that women are having worldwide. They are one of the largest non-profit women's organizations in the world annually touching the lives of more than 17 million women. This is staggering! Women on six continents in over 170 nations meet to carry out their mission which is "To help restore and mobilize women around the world. To promote gender reconciliation in the body of Christ as God designed. To amplify awareness of Global concerns from a biblical perspective." Through these forerunning women, the Gospel and its application is being carried out with courage and compassion and has been for the past forty years. Aglow is one snapshot of what God is doing through women around the world who are hearing Father's call to arise into their place in His kingdom. There are many other ministries and organizations that God is using to birth the restoration of women in the earth. To deny the value of what they are doing is to be blinded by the prejudice of false religious mindsets.

Women by the millions are hearing God, and the result will be ultimately glorious. Side by side with men they form the body of Christ—the new man in the earth who is also the bride of Christ. Sound confusing? Being one flesh means the man and the woman enjoy completeness together in order to fulfill God's purposes. In the physical, a man and a woman in union produce sons and daughters. In the spiritual, man and woman in union in the body of Christ laboring together sharing the Gospel are able to see the birthing of sons and daughters of God.

This is the season for women to hear who God says they are. They need to hear it in their spirit and let the seed of the truth product its fruit. Once a woman hears what Father has to say about her future, the warrior heart in her beckons her to say "Yes Lord!" This is the season that the power of Eden is being restored to the daughters of Eve. It is their inheritance through the cross of Christ. It is part of the restoration that is occurring. The Church is not just men

> **This is the season that the power of Eden is being restored to the daughters of Eve.**

with women tagging along. The Church is all the redeemed walking side by side at the foot of the cross regardless of gender, age, ethnicity, or economic position (Gal. 3:28).

Women, it is vital that you hear what Jesus says to you and about you. It is so important that you soak your soul and spirit in the Word of God. Through the Word, restoration takes place. Something that was lost in Eden can be established again in your heart. God's Word fills you with the truth of who you really are in Christ. When the dust is settled and all is said and done, it will be your acceptance of what God says about you that will make a great difference in your life. There is such protection, security, and acceptance within the Word of God for you as a woman. The power to restore is within the Word itself. Both men and women need to have their minds renewed by the whole counsel of God's Word.

I challenge men to lend the power of your voice to assist in the restoration of all things—especially the voice of women. Peter announced on the Day of Pentecost that daughters and handmaidens would begin using their voices prophetically. It's been almost two thousand years; let's get into agreement with what Peter told us God was going to do!

Chapter Thirteen
The Holy Spirit, Joyce Meyer & Oswald Chambers

There are two kinds of people: those who say to God, Thy will be done, and those to whom God says, All right, then, have it your way. - C. S. Lewis

~

Concrete blocks and men's heads sometimes appear to be made out of the same material. I have found, however, that God has a sledgehammer, and He knows how to swing it to get His message through my thick skull. One of the most powerful times He has ever spoken to me, He did so through a woman. At the time, it signaled a big change in my thinking.

It was around 3:00 A.M. on a Thursday morning in mid-July 1998 when I awakened. I knew that the Lord had awakened me. The previous day had fueled me with a desire to have more time to devote myself to prayer and ministry of the Word. Stanley Adair, the owner of our local Christian television station, had shared with me about his transition from the business world to full-time ministry. I admired Stanley's faith and determination. He had gone through a three year process of applying with the FCC to get his station on the air. His faith had become sight. Now here I was in the middle of the night struggling with the thoughts of resigning the pastorate at First Baptist Church and entering into…. Only God could finish that sentence, and I needed Him to finish it for me.

I can't explain it, but I had been sensing that I was supposed to minister to the body of Christ at large. The last year had been filled with so much change. I had gone from a desperate pastor ready to quit to having an encounter with the Holy Spirit that changed everything. The person I had been just over a year earlier would have had trouble fellowshipping with the person I had now become. God had required me to burn a lot of the theological boxes I had built. I had accepted that other people in other denominations also loved Jesus and were actually used by Him to build His kingdom. I had repented to the congregation I pastored and the ministers and men of the local chapter of Promise Keepers in our city. I even went on the local radio station and asked the whole city to forgive me for the times I had preached that caused believers to look down upon their fellow brothers and sisters in Christ. Things had radically changed in my life. Prayer was a delight and not drudgery. The Bible had come to life as never before for me. I enjoyed ministry. Even the warfare was in proper perspective. I felt equipped to win. It was so awesome! But this most recent stirring had me wondering about what was to happen next.

As I lay there awake in the middle of the night, I began talking with my Heavenly Father about these promptings and desires. Little did I know, He was about to do something that I had not thought He would ever do. He was going to use a woman to give direction to me and my entire family. So, at 3:00 in the morning, I started talking to God.

I said *"Lord, this doesn't make sense. Both of our vehicles have over 100,000 miles on them. We don't have our own home. We wouldn't have a place to live. We would have no income, health insurance, life insurance. We live in a parsonage, and we don't even have our own stove or refrigerator."*

Immediately, I was interrupted by the Holy Spirit who spoke,

"God is bigger than a refrigerator."

Well, He had me there. I felt scolded by the Lord. Of course, God is bigger than a refrigerator. If God wasn't bigger than a refrigerator, I really was in trouble.

In your praying to the Lord, have you ever said something really stupid? I mean "Daahh!!" And as soon as you said it, you realized it was stupid? It's like you start grabbing for the words as soon as they depart from the tip of your tongue, but you can't catch them. I guess we are all guilty at times of blabbing and then grabbing. Well that's what I did next. I said something very stupid to the Lord.

In response to His reminder to me that He was bigger than a refrigerator, I reacted by saying:

"But Lord, You don't understand! I have four children and this decision doesn't just affect me, it affects their futures." (Woops! Commence grabbing!)

Like engaging in a tennis match which I was destined to lose, the Holy Spirit immediately returned my verbal volley by gently reminding me,

"Your children's futures are in my hands."

Wow! I had accused my Father of not knowing what He was doing. I realize that I was speaking out of emotion—it sure wasn't a faith confession. I was taken aback by the Spirit's reply because His correction was so filled with compassion. Instead of lecturing me on the stupidity of what I had just said, He simply assured me that God would take care of my children. As He does so often, God looked beyond my fault and saw my need. He knew I needed to know that my babies would be all right. I already knew this was true as a matter of Bible "knowledge", but now I had a fresh word from God spoken into my spirit. I was now reminded and reassured in the depth of my spirit that the greatest thing I could do for my kids was to live in the will of God.

I remember a former pastor of mine who went to the foreign mission field saying, "I would rather my kids be on the mission field in the will of God under God's care than back here in the states out of the will of God under my care".

God was confronting me in the middle of this July night. He was not allowing me to wade into the waters of worry as I often did when thinking of pursuing this growing sense of His call in my life. As I edged into the waters of worry, this time He stopped me. He was clearly and verbally showing me the shallowness of all my concerns. I was using my compassion for my children as a challenge to my Heavenly Father that His compassion and care could not meet the standards that I felt my compassion and care were meeting. I did not think this way with intention but just the same the Lord helped me to see the conclusion of my thinking. This decision that seemed so filled with unanswered questions created a struggle within me. It was the struggle of faith and fear. All of us from time to time find ourselves in the ring with the strongman FEAR. He is so intimidating. His "what ifs" can paralyze us. Yet, the revelation that Father God loves us and will take care of us will topple him every day of the week.

I lay motionless in my bed for some time just thinking things through--processing this exchange with the Lord. Finally after thorough consideration, my heart in surrender cried out,

"Lord, you know I'll do what you tell me. I want to obey you and experience all you have for me. Lord I need to know for certain what you want me to do. Do you want me to stay or step out? Stay or step out? Stay or step out?"

"Stay or step out? Stay or step out?" kept coming up out of my spirit. I repeated this phrase eight or nine times, and then the Holy Spirit broke into my question with,

"Watch Joyce Meyer this morning, and you'll get your answer."

If you knew my past, you would realize that this directive showed how much miraculous change had already occurred in my life. It was just a few years earlier that I was laughing with my other seminary buddies as our professor talked about those "floozies" who had the audacity to stand behind a pulpit and preach God's Word. Now, here I was, Mr. Conservative Baptist, doctor's degree, First Church pastor, being told by God to go listen to a WOMAN to get the word that I needed for a major life shifting decision with which I was struggling. To show you how much I had already changed, I was excited about hearing what Joyce

Meyer would say in her broadcast. The Lord had already broken down a lot of my pride and arrogance and narrow mindedness about women in ministry. I am ashamed of some of the things I used to believe and think.

Joyce Meyer ministers through radio, television, and conferences. She has a very practical preaching and teaching style that is life changing. It is where the rubber meets the road. I remember years earlier, in my more judgmental days, hearing her on the radio ministering God's Word. I thought this woman preaches like she thinks it's really all right for her to preach. Interestingly, I kept listening to her but only when I was in the car alone. I would not have admitted it to anyone. Isn't it amazing how blind we can be? Obviously, even then my spirit was moving me to receive from Joyce, but

> **The Lord had already broken down a lot of my pride and arrogance and narrow mindedness about women in ministry.**

my mind would war against it. After my encounter with the Holy Spirit, however, my wife and I together started occasionally watching her television program. We were so hungry to learn how to live life in the Spirit, and Joyce would feed us.

The *Life in the Word* program aired in our area on cable at 5:30 A.M. on television. It had been a couple of weeks since we had watched the broadcast, but I was eager to watch it on this particular July morning.

It was about 5:00 A.M., and I lay there thinking, *"I'm about to find out if this was God or not speaking to me. In just a little bit, I will know if I have been imagining all of this or not.* I was about to discover that the Lord had set me up once again.

I lay there till 5:20 A.M. at which time I got up and heated some water for coffee. I was very interested in what was going to happen through the *Life in the Word* broadcast which would be airing shortly. I was determined to watch with rapt attention lest I miss God's answer to whether I should stay or step out. Maybe Joyce would mention or say something that would give me some insight as to what God wanted me to do. While the water was boiling, I woke up Mikki to watch the broadcast with me. I did not have the time to explain to her the importance of our watching this particular program on this particular day. I went back to the kitchen and made two cups of French vanilla cappuccino for Mikki and me. I walked into the den, handed Mikki her cup of coffee and then I flipped on the T.V. Little did I know that I was about to experience one of the most specific answers to prayer that I have ever experienced. Remember, I had asked the Lord, "Do you want me to stay or step out? Stay or step out? Stay or step out?" As I sat down on the couch, the *Life in the Word* broadcast was coming on. The first thing that happened on the program was a little intro where Joyce Meyer pointed her finger directly into the TV camera and said as if directly to me,

"God wants you to step out!"

I was stunned. I exploded into tears! I sounded like a bawling calf. I could not regain my composure.
Mikki looked at me with deep concern and said,

"What in the world is wrong with you?"

I couldn't even speak so that she could understand me. While snubbing, crying, and bawling, I told her that I had been praying and the Lord told me to watch Joyce Meyer, and I would find out if He wanted me to stay or step out. As I settled down a bit more, I told her about my conversation with the Lord. We both sat and listened as Joyce taught an entire lesson about staying in the boat where it was comfortable or stepping out and walking on water. It was one of the most absolutely amazing answers to prayer I have ever experienced. God had set me up. He had Stanley Adair stir my spirit telling about how God had provided for him to transition into a life of faith. He had awakened me in the middle of the night and caused His Spirit in me to stir my spirit to pray a certain thing. Then He responded by directing me to watch a program that had more than likely been planned months earlier that contained the match that would set off the gunpowder that

God had been pouring into me, and He used a woman—
Joyce Meyer—to strike the match. Wow! As a matter of fact,
leave the "Wow!" off. Let's pray that all we guys will get to
the place we are not caught off guard, surprised, and
amazed that God used a woman to do something
spectacular. Let's just be amazed that God would use any of
us and grateful that He can use all of us.

To cap it off, after Joyce's broadcast concluded the Holy
Spirit then spoke again saying,

"Now read Oswald Chambers devotional for today."

I went and got my Oswald Chambers devotional and read
what he wrote about radical obedience. What he had
written years ago now spoke specifically to my heart. This
was the second witness in the last few moments that
powerfully confirmed "what" I was to do. I had no doubt
that God had spoken. I was to step out. I now knew "what"
was supposed to happen--I just needed to know "when" it
was to happen. Was I to do it immediately? Was I to wait
until further confirmation? I have learned through the years
that timing is very important when it comes to the will of
God. Once you know "what" God wants you to do, you
then need to know "when" God wants you to do it. So I
made the decision that I was going to "step out" in faith and
follow God into the unknown. I would simply trust God to
give me a clear green light as to when I should resign the

pastorate and minister to the wider body of Christ. I knew that He had led me to First Baptist and that He would clearly communicate the time I needed to go. However, I now knew that it was just a matter of time until the Lord would lead me to take a big step of faith. The next spring the Lord spoke to us that it was time to take the step. We stepped out leaving all visible means of support and income. It was one of the best decisions we have ever made in our lives. Leaving where we were was difficult, and we still love the people there, but it was also one of the biggest decisions we have ever made it our lives—and God used a powerful woman of God to speak to me. He knows how to break down our man-made barriers of resistance. He spoke to me through Joyce Meyer! It was more than a powerful coincidence; it was God breaking me down my mindsets so He could break me out.

Joyce Meyer, Jane Hansen, Beth Moore, Stasi Eldredge, Wendy Alec, Heidi Baker, Karen Wheaton, Paula White, Cindy Jacobs, Kay Arthur, Ann Graham Lotz, Sherri Rose Shepperd, Shirley Dobson, Barbara Wentroble, Barbara Yoder, Robin McGraw and many others are living proof that women's voices in the body of Christ are beginning to have more impact than in other generations. No, these are not radical feminists calling for the overthrow of the role of men in our culture. Neither are these voices that are advocating that there are no differences between the man and the woman. Simply put, these are voices of women who have been anointed of God to influence culture toward God and His kingdom. We argue over how to classify them.

Preachers?--Teachers?--Prophetesses?

They are messengers of their Daddy God. We make war over which pigeon hole we are going to stuff them into. We make war over which camp we desire to affiliate them with.

Are they Baptist?--Methodist?--Charismatic?

We attempt to define them by the airwaves their voices may be heard upon.

TBN?--CBN?--Daystar?--SkyAngel?--God TV?--Word?

Our first response to a person's voice, man or woman, should be based upon how they are living and what they are saying. If it is a message from God, then we should be satisfied and grateful for whomever God uses to deliver it— male or female.

Chapter Fourteen
The Battle Over the Seed

A baby is God's opinion that life should go on. —*Carl Sandburg*

~

It is clear from a reading of the entire Bible that there is a battle over the seed. We are told that God created the seed with the power to reproduce.

Gen 1:11 Then God said, "Let the earth bring forth grass, the herb that yields seed, and the fruit tree that yields fruit according to its kind, whose seed is in itself, on the earth"; and it was so.... 13 So the evening and the morning were the third day.

Notice the terms, **"according to its kind"** and **"whose seed is in itself."** This is what a seed is and does; it is a vehicle of life that reproduces after its own kind. God placed the seed in the ground on the third day of creation. I believe this in itself is a picture of the resurrection of Jesus who was to be the promised Seed of the human race who would be raised from the dead on the third day.

The seed represents the future harvest and the coming generations. There is war over the seed. For the farmer, if there is no seed for the field, there will ultimately be no food for the table. For the cattleman, if there is no seed, in a matter of years he will have no herd. For the human family, without the seed, we would vanish from the earth thus missing the fulfillment of God's mandate and purposes. The seed is very important. When God made the decree He did in Genesis 3:15, He was testifying and prophesying that He would watch over the woman's seed until the day came when One would arise to fulfill the promise of the overthrow of Satan's kingdom. War followed this Word from God. As the history of the Old Testament unfolded, God narrowed the promise. He began to define the family lines that the seed would emerge from. Abraham, Isaac, Jacob, Judah and David were all given assurances that it would be through their lineage that the whole world would be blessed. The Gospel writers even give us the genealogies to provide the genetic trail of fulfillment for these promises. Interestingly the descendents of Abraham have been the target of hate, jealousy, and war due to the promises of God given to them. In Moses' day, Pharaoh decreed the death of the sons born in Israel.

Ex 1:16 and he said, "When you do the duties of a midwife for the Hebrew women, and see them on the birthstools, if it is a son, then you shall kill him; but if it is a daughter, then she shall live."

There was a lot of supernatural phenomenon that surrounded the birth of Jesus. Angelic appearances to shepherds, wise men seeing a star, and Simeon and Anna prophesying were all very unusual, and certainly their stories began to be spread. When news began to spread that a new King was being born in Israel, the enemy once again struck hoping to extinguish the One who was prophesied to come. As in the days of Moses, the enemy worked to issue a judicial decree through human government in the hopes of overriding God's decree made to the woman. It is important to realize that Satan is full of pride. He detests what God spoke over his future in the garden when Eve fell. He is still fighting to circumvent God's plans in all of our lives. He hates the Seed of God. If you are a believer, you carry the seed, and the devil hates you too (John 10:10).

He spread his hatred through King Herod when Jesus was born. Herod had a plan to find out specifically who this child was. When his plan failed, he simply ordered the execution of all the baby boys in the region.

Matt 2:16 ...and he sent forth and put to death all the male children who were in Bethlehem and in all its districts, from two years old and under, according to the time which he had determined from the wise men.

The Lord was at work watching over the promised Seed. He warned the wise men in a dream to have nothing to do with Herod, and then He warned Joseph by means of a dream to leave the region.

Matt 2:13 …an angel of the Lord appeared to Joseph in a dream, saying, "Arise, take the young Child and His mother, flee to Egypt, and stay there until I bring you word; for Herod will seek the young Child to destroy Him."

It is the nature of Satan to steal and destroy the seed. God declared a word over the serpent, and the word He declared carried the power to seal Satan's doom. This is the nature of the Word of God; it functions like a seed. It contains the power to reproduce the promise it contains. The enemy attacks the Word of God. The Word of God is a weapon in our hand because it contains the future promise for each of us. This is the power of making decrees with the promises of God.

The Word of God in our mouth is like a sword in the hand of a soldier. It is even called the sword of the Spirit in Ephesians 6:17. When we declare what God has said it carries weight because the power to fulfill what we speak is within the very Word of God that we have sown. Just like a seed in the ground when sown takes root and bears fruit, so does the Word of God. This is the reason the devil attacks the Word. Jesus told a parable about a sower, the seed, and the soils. In this teaching, He clearly

> **The Word of God in our mouth is like a sword in the hand of a soldier.**

tells us what Satan is up to when it comes to the Word of God.

Matt 13:19 When anyone hears the word of the kingdom, and does not understand it, then the wicked one comes and snatches away what was sown in his heart. This is he who received seed by the wayside.

The focus of this book is about a Word from God in which God said that He was going to use women and their seed to be the enemies of Satan; therefore, Satan has launched all out war against women and against her womb in the hopes of destroying the Word from God. The Word was ultimately fulfilled in the birth, ministry, death, burial, and resurrection of Jesus. However, Satan's battle against God's Word and against women and their wombs did not stop with

> **Satan has launched all out war against women and against her womb in the hopes of destroying the Word from God.**

Jesus. Our victory was settled with Jesus, but we still battle to enforce that victory in our own lives, circumstances, and sphere of influence.

The whole abortion issue is about the seed which is provided by the man and the womb which is provided by the woman and the future generation which is the fruit of the womb. In America alone there have been over 47 million abortions since it was legalized in the now infamous Roe vs Wade Case of 1973.[26] On a global scale the number of reported abortions has reached close to one billion babies.[27] Take China, for example, where women are forced to have abortions after they have had one child. This is a case of mandated murder. Just like he did in the days of Pharaoh and Herod, the enemy has worked in our nation through human government and brought about a decree of death over our unborn through our own Supreme Court. *The demonic purpose is the same as it has always been—to stop or slow down the promises and purposes of God.* Think of the unborn ministers of the Gospel, the apostles, prophets, evangelists, pastors, and teachers whose voices will not be heard because of this unjust legislation. Think about the impact on global evangelization that this has caused. This is the spirit of Antichrist at work. Daniel prophesied of such a one who would work against the saints of God.

Dan 7:25 He shall speak pompous words against the Most High, Shall persecute the saints of the Most High, And shall intend to change times and law.

Notice that Daniel saw this wicked personality speaking arrogantly, persecuting the saints, with the intention of changing times and laws. This is the nature of antichrist spirit. It works to throw off the timing of God's purposes by working through human government to change times and law. I firmly believe this happened in 1973 because God has intended great plans of harvest and revival for the emerging generation. Abortion is the unwarranted taking of human life, but it is also the purposeful interfering with God's plans for the next generation. We should all pray diligently and stand strongly against the spirit that is behind abortion. We must see its overthrow in our culture in order to have the full measure of the blessing of God upon our nation and the nations.

I recently felt called of God to lead a prayer journey around the entire State of Alabama in which I live. So in October 2006, a small band of believers and I set out together. We traveled over 1600 miles in a little over two days to the four corners of the State. Our last stop was in the center of the state in the capital city of Montgomery. We had researched and addressed a number of historical and spiritually significant issues that related to our state at each place we planned to stop and pray We refer to this process as spiritual mapping. The last corner of the state in which we prayed was the northeast corner. We arrived there after nightfall so we ended up praying in the dark under a night light. Kevin Creekmore, our resident historian and spiritual mapper, shared with us that we were praying in a historically strategic location. We were near the entry point of the state where most of the immigrants moved south from the northern and eastern states. It was also located near the Trail of Tears where the Native American Indians were forced to walk away from their homes. At the root of this exodus was the Indian Removal Act of 1836. It is realized today that the event reeked of governmental fraud and deceit in removing the Indians from lands that had been previously documented as belonging to them. Families were forced to leave by gunpoint and in many cases with just the clothes on their backs. Estimates are that more than 4000 of them died before reaching Oklahoma. While we prayed that night, I had an unusually intense experience in intercession. Those schooled in intercessory terminology would call it identificational intercession. I began praying in an unknown tongue, and it became very pronounced and intense. I personally believe I was praying in a Native American tongue of some sort. People who were there also indicated to me that it sounded like a tribal language of some sort. I then experienced a vision in which I saw a Native American woman standing by the bank of what I knew to be the Tennessee River. I also knew the vision was something that had taken place during the Trail of Tears. The woman was crying. As she stood there weeping, her tears were falling into the river. I knew that she was weeping because a group of white men had seized her and had stripped her baby out of her arms and thrown the child into the river. She had lost her child. It was so intense. I could feel what this woman felt. It was as if her emotions became my emotions. There was a deep grief and sorrow that filled my heart. I began weeping uncontrollably trying to articulate to the people with me what I was seeing. Then I heard the Spirit of the Lord say, *"It is no different today. The government has made a decision that has caused people to throw their babies to their deaths. There have not been enough tears that have fallen into the river. I am going to release a spirit of repentance over this state and when the tears begin to fall then the river level will rise. When you see the rivers in Alabama begin to flood, you will know the spirit of repentance is doing its work, and things are about to shift. It is about the babies. It is about the babies."*

Words cannot describe to you how I felt during this experience. It was so serious and sobering. Everyone knew that God was doing something. It was a while before I regained my composure and for several days afterward, each time I would try to discuss it I would break down weeping. It is about the babies—the seed.

I encourage you reader to see a parallel in all of this. We should cherish life in the womb, and we should cherish the life contained in God's Word to us. The two work together to bring about the fulfillment of God's plans and purposes. Many of you have been given personal prophetic words. Realize that true prophetic words contain the life of your future in them. As such they are weapons in your hand to keep you on track with God's plans and purposes. Isn't this what Paul told young Timothy?

1 Tim 1:18 This charge I commit to you, son Timothy, according to the prophecies previously made concerning

you, that by them you may wage the good warfare , 19 having faith and a good conscience, which some having rejected, concerning the faith have suffered shipwreck,

Timothy was told that he would stay on course and avoid shipwreck by waging warfare using the prophetic words spoken over him previously.

Dear Sisters in Christ, you have a Word that God has spoken over you. He decreed that you would be Satan's enemy. He decreed that your seed would be Satan's enemy. He decreed that the seed of woman would crush the serpent's head. Jesus is the promised Seed. He is in you. In His name, begin to decree that your life and the lives of the seed that have been carried and developed in your womb will also be Satan's enemy. You know this is God's will and desire—Decree it! Do warfare with it! I will share with you how to do this in the next chapter.

Chapter Fifteen
The Power of a Mother's Decree

There is in every true woman's heart a spark of heavenly fire
which lies dormant in the broad daylight of prosperity; but which
kindles up and beams and blazes in the dark hour of adversity. —
Washington Irving[28]

~

The power invested in women by God to be the bearers of
the kings and governors of the next generation is an
incredible thought. William Ross Wallace in the mid-1860's
poetically hit upon this in his now famous lines:

They say that man is mighty,
He governs land and sea,
He wields a mighty scepter
O'er lesser powers that be;
But a mightier power and stronger
Man from his throne has hurled,
For the hand that rocks the cradle
Is the hand that rules the world.[29]

The love a mother has for her child and the power of a
mother's prayer are both very remarkable. Every mother
carries a seed from the father of the child in her womb until
the child is born. Mothers have been entrusted with the safe

keeping of the next generation. Mothers are typically and historically the greatest influencers of the next generation. I encourage women to know that they can take the principle of Genesis 3:15 and apply it to their own seed. The decree that God made over the serpent also becomes a weapon in the mouth of a mother. Let me share a story to illustrate this truth.

Tears filled the eyes of our friend as she shared the burden on her heart for her son. Mikki and I listened as she and her husband shared that they felt God had a call on the life of their son, but he was running. The precious couple is involved in an international ministry, yet the good news they traveled around the world to share with others had not found its way into the heart of their own son. He had made choices that had him on a road that led in the opposite direction. Their concern was not based on embarrassment; they cared for their son's soul. As I listened, my heart went out for them and for their son. I felt anger toward the enemy rise up within me. These were good people who loved God. They had invested their lives in the kingdom. They were good parents who were careful not to neglect their children. They were not legalistic or overbearing. One of their little lambs was becoming prey to Satan. It is difficult for parents when their children reject the truths that are the most important to them.

I began sharing with them about a weapon from the Word that I felt the Lord had shown me concerning the power of a mother's prayer. I looked into the mother's eyes and began sharing. Let me speak to you what I spoke to her that day in regard to prayers for her son. It is truth I have shared with other mothers as well.

Do you realize that God's Word teaches us that the enemy always comes after the seed of the woman? It is true all through the Bible. Children whom God has ordained to do something special and significant seem to be the special targets of the enemy. When Eve was deceived in the Garden by the serpent, it was like God said, "This is going to cost you!" Think about what God told the serpent. He decreed over the serpent that from now on this woman whom you have deceived is going to be your enemy. Not only will she be your enemy, but her seed will be your enemy. In other words, God decreed that the woman and her seed would be a weapon in His hand to topple Satan's kingdom. Of course, this promise was fulfilled in Christ. I encourage you to take this principle and apply it to your situation. Satan is coming against your seed, right? What was God's Word to the woman? You are going to be Satan's enemy, right? And your seed is going to be Satan's enemy, right? Decree it! Decree that your son is going to serve the Lord and be a force against Satan. Decree that your seed is blessed of the Lord and that the power of the enemy's deception will not hold him. Decree that your son will be a weapon in God's hand to topple Satan's empire. It is a good thing to be Satan's enemy; decree that your son is going to be Satan's enemy. Is it not true that Jesus came to destroy all the works of the Devil? Is it not true that you are in Christ? Is it not true that the woman's Seed, Christ, has set you free? Then you can destroy the works of the Devil. Your seed can destroy the works of the Devil. Agree with God concerning your son's destiny. Decree it for your seed.

As I shared these words, I could see the light bulb of revelation flip on in her spirit and mind. Her eyes widened

> **Decree that your seed is blessed of the Lord and that the power of the enemy's deception will not hold him.**

as she excitedly grasped the truth of what I had spoken. I asked her to pray and decree the truth of God's Word over her son's life. She prayed a beautiful faith filled prayer claiming her son's destiny for the purposes of God. After the "Amen" was spoken, it was apparent that there was peace and the couple felt they had a new weapon to use in their warfare for their son. They left to return to their home state. I spoke with them over the course of the next few months and would ask about their son on each of those occasions. Their confidence in what God was going to do was apparent. About six months later, my brother called and left me a message. His son had been saved and was scheduled to be baptized. He was on fire for God, and they were ecstatic. I rejoiced when I heard this, and I delighted in the incredible power of prayer and in the goodness of God. When we decree that we agree with what God says, powerful things can happen.

Allow me to share with you a passage of Scripture from the book of Job. It is from a section where one of Job's friends is accusing Job of wrong doing. Even though Eliphaz is later rebuked for his attitude toward Job, what he shares about decreeing is consistent with the truths found in many other passages in the Bible. Here are the verses:

Job 22:28 You will also declare a thing,
And it will be established for you;
So light will shine on your ways.
29 When they cast you down, and you say, 'Exaltation will come!'
Then He will save the humble person.
30 He will even deliver one who is not innocent;
Yes, he will be delivered by the purity of your hands."

Notice some of the truths in this passage:

1. There is a time and place for you to declare a thing.

This word "declare" is the Hebrew word *gazar*.[30] It is translated "decree" in the King James Version. It has the idea of cutting a covenant. It is at times used in a judicial sense of a command or order or the releasing of authority. There are times for the believer to get into

> **Sometimes we are guilty of moaning and groaning when we need to be decreeing and declaring.**

agreement with God's Word and begin to release it with authority into his/her situation. Sometimes we are guilty of moaning and groaning when we need to be decreeing and declaring. Jesus taught us that we have the authority to bind and loose and to remit and retain (Matt. 18:18-19). He also taught about the power of agreement in our prayers (Matt. 18:19-20). He gives us the assurance that when we are in agreement about the will and Word of God that He is in our midst. When we voice defeat, we agree with the enemy. When we voice victory, we agree with our God. Be careful who you agree with! It is important to note that earlier Eliphaz mentioned that it was God's Word that should fill Job's heart.

Job 22:22 Receive, please, instruction from His mouth, And lay up His words in your heart.

When God's Word fills our hearts, then it can be powerfully declared out of our mouths. It must be a heart declaration resting moved by confidence in God. A mere intellectual agreement will not do. The heart must be filled with a faith that rests on a deep trust in God's ability to do and God's willingness to do.

God created the entire universe by declaring His Word out of His mouth. He spoke, and what He spoke was established. Have you ever thought about the fact that the creation first existed in the mind and heart of God? He saw it before He spoke it. What existed as potential with Him came into actuality through what He spoke.

You and I are created in the image of God. Part of the image of God that exists within us is the ability to see things before they exist. We call this imagination. I like to refer to it as image-i-nation. In other words, the imagination that you and I possess is part of the package of being made in the image of God. Now it can be used in a polluted way because of our sin nature. But it is still something we possess of God's image in us. We can see the potential of things. We can see how things could be different if changes were made. We can perceive new ideas, inventions, and methods of doing things.

The first thing that Adam did after God created him was to begin declaring names over the animals. The Bible says that whatever he called them is what they were. Though corrupted, this is still operative today. However, when we are cleansed by the blood of Jesus and speak God's Word in God's time in God's way, then we see the unfolding of God's will in the earth. Isn't this

> **The enemy does not want you going around repeating what God has said. The Word of God is powerful.**

how Jesus taught us to pray, "Thy kingdom come, thy will be done. On Earth as it is in Heaven"? Literally, the Scripture is grammatically written to be the utterance of a command, "Kingdom of God, come! Will of God, be done! On earth as it is in Heaven (Matt. 6:10)." It is an exhilarating thought to realize that God wants us to invoke His will here by declaring it through our mouths. The enemy does not want you going around repeating what God has said. The Word of God is powerful.

In the Gospel of Mark, Jesus clearly teaches that what we say is important and carries power.

Mark 11:22 So Jesus answered and said to them, "Have faith in God. 23 For assuredly, I say to you, whoever says to this mountain , 'Be removed and be cast into the sea,' and does not doubt in his heart, but believes that those things he says will be done, he will have whatever he says.

The book of Proverbs also reminds us of the truth that we can speak death or life and will receive the benefits or consequences of what we speak.

Proverbs 18:20 A man's stomach shall be satisfied from the fruit of his mouth; From the produce of his lips he shall be filled. 21 Death and life are in the power of the tongue, And those who love it will eat its fruit.

When we declare God's Word, we are declaring words of life and as a result we reap blessing. Charles Spurgeon reminded us that we do not have to defend the Word of God. He said it was like a lion in a cage—all you had to do was to let it out. This is so true. When you begin releasing the Word of God, it will do its work, and the enemy knows it. Therefore, hell trembles before the mouth that releases the will of heaven into the earth. Dutch Sheets in his powerful book, *Intercessory Prayer*, reminds us that there are some things that God desires to do here on earth that He does not do until someone prays. Declaring and decreeing are weapons that are given us to use in our arsenal of prayer. There is a time and place that the believer needs to declare the Word of God into his/her circumstances. The Word of God created the world; it is powerful enough to change it!

2. What you declare will be established for you.

All through Scripture we see God moving to perform His Word (Jer. 1:12). When we get into alignment with the Word of God, it brings things around us into alignment. God desires to perform His will in the earth. His Word contains His will. When we declare God's Word, He backs it up. This is what happens when the Gospel is preached. When someone responds to the Gospel, God backs it up and saves them. He establishes the truth of the Gospel in their hearts.

President Lyndon Johnson once said, *"If two men agree on everything, you may be sure that one of them is doing the thinking."*[31] He said this to encourage us to do our own thinking. We should, however, let God do the thinking for us. We must pray that our minds will be conformed to His. It is important to get God's mind on a matter regardless of what everyone else may be saying. This is what true wisdom is—seeing life from God's point of view. He is the only One who sees all the facts and facets of a situation. Father knows best. His Word and His Holy Spirit work together to give us His point of view in every circumstance we face.

God honors His Word. He watches over it to perform it. He is looking for people here in the earth whose hearts are perfect toward Him through whom He can show Himself strong (2 Chron. 16:9). The good news is that God is omnipotent, so if we will obediently declare what He wants declared, He has the power to bring it to pass. When He spoke to the serpent, was He not basically saying, *"I am going to partner with this woman, and you will begin eating shoe leather when it happens!"?* Father God is our model for decreeing. In the middle of the first failure in the human family, He began declaring victory would arise out the ashes. This is a basic premise throughout the Bible—*Good triumphs over evil* (Rom. 12:1, Rom. 8:28)! When you decree the Word of God, you are planting a seed. When the seed comes up it will reproduce after its own kind. You will reap what you have sown. Sow words of life into your children and your circumstances.

3. When we declare and God begins establishing, more revelation comes.

The next thing to be seen in this passage in Job is that light shines on your way.

**Job 22:28 You will also declare a thing,
And it will be established for you;
So light will shine on your ways.**

The reason light comes is because you have declared it. It is important to understand this. You see it by faith in God's Word to start with. You declare it out of your mouth to proceed with it. Then you begin seeing it in the natural. Light begins to shine on your ways. The way to break darkness is to release light. The Psalmist says,

Ps 119:130 The entrance of Your words gives light;…

We need light inside our heart before we can release light through our mouths. But once we are able to do this, then light begins to shine upon our ways. You have to "see" before you can see. As we begin to see spiritually, we are able to release decrees so that we can see circumstantially. When a woman begins to decree that her child shall be Satan's enemy, and she really sees it through the Word and in her spirit, then the light will begin to shine upon her child. Where the light shines, darkness flees.

Jesus also taught that when we respond to truth, freedom comes (John 8:31-32). It is very important to respond revelation when it is given. When we do, good things follow.

4. We can decree a change in our future circumstances.

I love the clarity of the next verse.

Job 20:29 When they cast you down, and you say, 'Exaltation will come!' Then He will save the humble person.

Wow! When you are down, declare that "up" is coming. I know that there have been those who have abused "positive thinking", but there is no denying that we are to be people of positive speaking. The enemy wants you to agree with him. He wants you to say what he says. God wants you to agree with Him. He wants you to say what

> **When you are down, declare that "up" is coming.**

He says. Your choice! It will be in your trying times when you are tempted to agree with enemy. This is what the serpent did in the garden. He got Eve to agree with him. There is power in agreement. That power can operate in darkness or light. It is so important that we agree with what God says in His Word. Job 22:29 reminds us not to say what "they" are saying.

5. Humility precedes power in the declaring of God's Word.

Job 22:29...Then He will save the humble person.

If you think you can use God's Word in a prideful way, then think again. The decreeing of God's Word has to be done from an humble heart. The humble heart knows that it is God who must move in order for the mountain to move. He has told us to speak to the mountain, but the speaking must be from an humble heart or we might release a landslide in which we get buried instead of seeing the mountain moved. God resists the proud but gives grace to the humble (James 4:6). Grace is God's power given to us to do God's will. It is not God's will for any of us to be proud, so He will not give grace when we are. Pride always goes before a fall. As I heard one preacher say, "If you strut like a peacock one day, then you may be a feather duster the next."

When your heart is humble, then you can declare that exaltation will come, and God will save you. That is His promise. He will lift you up. He exalts the humble. The sure way out of a hole is stay low and declare God's Word contrary to what the enemy's

> **The humble heart knows that it is God who must move in order for the mountain to move.**

crowd is saying.

6. Your decree can deliver those who are not innocent.

This truth ought to crank your tractor and get you plowing. Can you tell I'm from the South? Read this verse slowly.

Job 22:30 He will even deliver one who is not innocent; Yes, he will be delivered by the purity of your hands."

This is definitely a verse that a praying mother should grab hold of for her wayward child. Woman of God, the Word says the Lord will deliver one who is not innocent by the purity of your hands. This motivates us to see that we can help people who are not living for the Lord. Our prayers can pave the way for them to come back to God. Of course they can refuse, but when we pray it lessens the resistance of the enemy and increases the receptivity of their hearts. We all have experienced the difference that is made in our lives when people are praying for us.

The world will tell you that your children are a lost cause. The enemy will accuse and say that they are too deep in darkness to ever love the light. Your own carnal mind will try to rise up and convince you that it is too late, that you are a failure, and your children are too far gone. You must not conform to the world. You must resist the devil. You must crucify your flesh and decree God's truth and hold onto it with all the faith you can muster. God spared you because of what Jesus did for you. His heart is to forgive. His heart is to go looking for the lost. He is looking for the prodigal to come home. Believe in the goodness and grace that fills the heart of your Father God. Believe that because of what Jesus has done for you, that you can also do something for your kids, and God will honor it. You are a joint heir with Christ. His blood has covered your sins. You have access through His blood into the presence of Father God. Learn to decree the will of God over the life of your child. God's heart is so redemptive in nature. Even when Eve stood guilty before Him, His plan was to use her to bring about the overthrow of Satan's plans and schemes. His heart is still filled with the same desires. He will work through you as you decree, pray, and walk in humility. Decree your children home in Jesus' Name! Yes, they have a will, but the Holy Spirit can influence them and your prayerful decrees can create a spiritual environment around them to help shift their hearts toward God. His Word is full of power. Release it over them! This is what Father God did when he released His decree to the serpent. He declared the comeback of the woman. He declared that she would arise in victory though her head was hanging in defeat. If Daddy God did it, why can't every believing parent do it?

> **Decree your children home in Jesus' Name!**

Chapter Sixteen
Women and the Cultural War

A sufficient measure of civilization is the influence of good women. -Ralph Waldo Emerson

~

Have you ever thought about the fact that Eve was perfect, yet she was deceived? She had no sin nature, yet she received one through being deceived. She was not deceived because of any inherent weakness. If it were due to inherent weakness, then God's proclamation that all He had made was good and very good was not true. At least we should all admit that at our very best we can be deceived. In other words, we might be guilty of seeing something differently than it really is. Could it be that we have been guilty of missing the mark on some of our mindsets concerning the women's issue? Just a question, but one we should venture to address.

If you think about it, *Eve* is just one letter off from *Even* and there has forever been a struggle with women coming up "even" with men. Well, almost forever, because in the beginning it was not so. Eve stood at Adam's side. They both were given dominion and authority. However, at the point of their committing sin, things began to change and a war has followed. What was intended as an eternal partnership of powerful unity that would birth God's plans in the earth became a divided household where a murder in the family occurred between the first two sons ever born (Genesis 4). One generation deep and there's murder in the first family.

Women have been fighting for the acceptance and respect of men since the day Adam and Eve left Eden. To put it bluntly, she has had to face the hordes of hell and fight her way through history. Even today in our civilized modern times, she still is the target of dumb blonde jokes, viewed as inferior by many, and seen as a sex object by others. Yet her voice is being heard as never before. She is walking the halls of Congress, sitting at the head of the conference tables at board meetings, performing heart surgery in hospitals, flying airliners into major airports, and even preaching from pulpits formerly occupied by men only. I believe it is a new day for women. They are beginning to step into the places of destiny originally intended for them. Some have stepped into places that have resulted in history making changes. It is difficult to biblically align with the radical ideology of the modern day feminist movement. However, one should not associate all the progress of the past generations with the ideology that drives the movement today. Noble women in the early days of the movement arose to address grievous and very discriminating issues. Their courage is to be commended.

The courageous women of history inspire the daughters of today so that they can arise and become world changers and history makers. Think of the chain of events ignited as a result of the courage of Rosa Parks in Montgomery, Alabama, in 1954. Her spark of courage lit a fire in so many people that it is seen by many to be the cornerstone event of the modern Civil Rights Movement. Examples of courageous women changing culture are strewn throughout the centuries for us to see and admire.

On January 6, 1412, the vibrant voice of a newborn baby girl could be heard crying out from a peasant's house in Domrémy, France. It was the voice of Joan of Arc, a peasant girl, who 17 years later along with her

> **The courageous women of history inspire the daughters of today so that they can arise and become world changers and history makers.**

family would be granted the status of nobility by Charles VII, King of France. Why such an honor? As a teenage girl on a mission from God, she became the voice that would thrust the armies of England out of various cities in France. In a day and time when women were more like slaves than equals, Joan was a girl who proved herself to be an unusual warrior among men. Her mystic experiences and indomitable spirit made her a force with which to be reckoned. Her voice released something that filled men's hearts with the fire to fight and win! As one might expect, she was hated by many. How dare a teenager give counsel to the religious and political elite! The fact that the teenager was a girl was even more humiliating to them. Joan increasingly became the target of political and religious forces that were hell-bent on stopping her—and they did. Before she saw the conclusion of too many years, her voice was silenced at the tender age of 19. She was tried, branded a heretic, and burned at the stake. In 1456, twenty-five years later, a retrial was held, and it was

"ruled that the original trial had been tainted by fraud, illegal procedures, and intimidation of both the defendant and many of the clergy who had taken part in the trial, and she was therefore described as a martyr by the Inquisitor."[32]

In 1920, the same year that the voices of women in America were liberated to be heard in the voting booths, Joan of Arc was canonized as a saint. Today, this courageous young woman branded a heretic is considered a saint by the religious leaders of the church that burned her alive. Things can change, and they are!

Let me share another example more contemporary and outside the scope of the church. During the Second World War, everyone worked and contributed to the war effort. Women played many significant roles in helping the U.S.A., and the allied powers experience victory. However, they were not always recognized for what they did. Consider the Women's Auxiliary Ferrying Service that became known as

WAFS. There were 1,074 women who went through training and graduated to fly airplanes across the US and Canada in order to deliver them to the troops who would use them in the war effort. Eleven of the women were killed during their training. Thirty-eight of them were killed during the course of the war. The first woman pilot to lose her life was Cornelia Fort who died in a mid-air crash in Abilene, Texas on March 21, 1943. Cornelia was honored to serve her country. As a matter of fact, upon her acceptance as a ferrying pilot she wrote a letter home which said, "the heavens have opened up and rained blessings on me. The army has decided to let women ferry ships, and I'm going to be one of them." On a historical marker near an airpark named after her in Nashville, Tennessee, are more of her own words, "I am grateful that my one talent, flying, was useful to my country."[33] Cornelia was the first woman on active military duty to give her life for her country in WWII. These women did not demand that they fly missions over Nazi Germany, they just wanted to contribute and do their part in helping our nation during a time of tremendous crisis. The WAFs freed up the male pilots to fly combat missions. These women had to fly aircraft that had never been flown before. They often had to fly in open cockpits in freezing weather using visual landmarks to guide them due to the absence of radios in the planes. These women pilots were responsible for ferrying 12,650 planes representing over 77 various types of aircraft from the factories where the planes were constructed to the airfields where they disembarked for the war. They were ultimately disbanded on December 20, 1944, after having faithfully and valiantly served their country. They had braved the cutting comments of the male pilots who constantly argued that a woman could not pilot an aircraft as well as a man, though the statistics proved otherwise. Sadly, the brave thirty-eight women who died for their country were not allowed the honor of receiving a military burial. They were considered civilians only. The American flag could not be draped on their funeral biers. This was not the first time that women were deemed ineligible for that which was freely given to men.

There are many stories of women showing their strength in a man's world. For example, Babe Ruth and Lou Gehrig of the New York Yankees were struck out back to back in a major league exhibition game in 1931 by a 17 year-old young lady named Jackie Mitchell.[34] She pitched for the Chattanooga Lookouts, a minor league AA team in Chattanooga, Tennessee. When Babe struck out it is reported that he *"kicked the dirt, called the umpire a few dirty names, gave his bat a wild heave, and stomped out to the Yank's dugout."* She was quickly pulled from the game after humiliating the two giants of baseball. She was also released (fired) from her contract shortly afterwards with the statement that baseball was too strenuous for a woman. There just was not a place for *her* talent among the men's world of baseball. When asked about women and baseball, Babe Ruth said,

"I don't know what's going to happen if they begin to let women in baseball. Of course, they will never make good. Why? Because they are too delicate. It would kill them to play ball every day."[35]

Have men looked down upon women as inferior? Yes! But some may ask, "Have educated and enlightened men done so?" Again, the answer is "Yes!" Consider what Grover Cleveland said just a little over 100 years ago after his second term as President of the United States of America and just a few years before women were finally given the right to vote.

"Sensible and responsible women do not want to vote. The relative positions to be assumed by man and woman in the working out of our civilization were assigned long ago by a higher intelligence than ours."[36]

President Cleveland shared his sentiment that God Himself determined that the voice of a woman should remain silent in regard to governmental issues. Yet before the Fall of man, Woman was given along with her husband dominion in the realm of Earth.

President Cleveland's comments simply reflected the thinking of his day. This mindset was not new. Over two hundred years ago, a decade before he became the first

Vice-President and the second President of the United States, John Adams wrote a letter in response to his self-educated and feisty bride Abigail in which he said, *"I must not write a word to you about politics, because you are a woman."*[37]

Abigail, however, was a woman who saw injustice in the way the voices of women were being disregarded. In one of her letters, she strongly asserts to her husband that he and the Continental Congress

> "...remember the ladies, and be more generous and favorable to them than your ancestors. Do not put such unlimited power into the hands of the Husbands. Remember all Men would be tyrants if they could. If particular care and attention is not paid to the Ladies [sic] we are determined to foment a Rebellion, and will not hold ourselves bound by any Laws in which we have no voice, or Representation."[38]

At the dawn of the forming of this great country, there were perhaps some very heated discussions concerning the fact that men should hear what women had to say on some issues other than cooking, children, and the weather. These sporadic written interchanges between John and Abigail Adams certainly give us a glimpse into the tensions that existed as this country was being founded. When the future

First Lady speaks of beginning a rebellion in the midst of a country that has just fought one, it's pretty serious. Abigail's words obviously spoke of the sentiments of other women as well. On June 4, 1919, the U.S. Congress passed the 19th amendment which gave women the right to vote. On August 18, 1920, after the amendment had been ratified by the 36th of 48 states, the people of Tennessee's vote put the amendment into the Constitution of the United States of America. Our citizenship finally agreed that the voice of women was to be recognized as important in making decisions that would govern this great nation. At

> **At that moment, a touch of Eden's former glory fell once again upon the voice of a woman.**

that moment, a touch of Eden's former glory fell once again upon the voice of a woman. She would have a voice in the affairs of governing the earth.

However, other states were slow in finally coming into agreement with the 19th Amendment. Though they had to abide by the law, they were reluctant in making it official in the documents of their states. Many of the remaining states took years to ratify the amendment. Their earlier votes had been to reject it. Through the years, they slowly, one by one, made the change. Finally, the 48th of the original forty-eight states, Mississippi, ratified the 19th Amendment on March 22, 1984, and placed it in their books. This shows it takes time to change cultural mindsets. The same struggle was witnessed over the issue of slavery which cost us so greatly. The blood of over 650,000 lives soaked the soil of our own nation before it was over. Yet, after the war, it was another hundred years before African Americans really got their day in court at the desk of President Lyndon Johnson when he signed into law the Civil Rights Act.

It did not mean that these former political leaders did not recognize the intrinsic value and honor of a woman, but it does reflect that they and most men of their day and most men of all time, tend to view a woman as inferior or at least that her role in society is less important than a man's. Mindsets are hard to describe, but they are so powerful. I have heard it said, *"A man persuaded against his will is of the same opinion still."* Yep, we can be stubborn as a mule. It is true that we have a change of mindsets through a change of our wills. We are certainly less eager to change our minds about something that has become so deeply engrained in our thinking. Earlier in my ministry a man shared with me, "Don't argue with people about religion, hunting dogs, or politics." Where I grew up, all three of these were hot buttons. Obviously, I have ignored some of this advice although I rarely discuss hunting dogs. Race and the role of women in culture are certainly hot buttons that seem to have no geographic bounds.

The struggle still continues in the mindsets of many Americans when it comes to the prejudice toward women and minorities. As with any struggle, there are always extremists. The extremist answer is always to hate those who stand in the way of change or to hate those who want the change. Extremism also denigrates moral judgment because the cause can become seen as more important than the truth. A wrong mindset becomes grounded in what one wants instead of what is true. This is always dangerous. For example, the modern war over abortion is presented as a woman's rights issue. But is it? The person paying the price is the human life in the womb. Who speaks for the unborn child?

The same motivation that served the righteous cause to give women the right to vote should apply to the child instead of the woman. The science of the womb increasingly is showing the validity of life in the womb. The latest 4D technology shows twins and triplets holding hands and bonding while still in the womb. Debates have raged over when life begins. Trying to pinpoint the first moment of viability is important. I firmly believe that life begins at conception. The sperm contains life, and the egg contains life even before conception. However, it is when the two come together that "human life" begins. Today, with the modern miracle of neonatal technology, prematurely born infants are living after 20-21 weeks in the womb. Fifty years ago the timeline of viability was at 30 weeks. By 25 years ago the viability timeline had dropped to 25 weeks. Today, a premature baby has survived at 20 weeks and several at

21 weeks.[39] Do these babies who can live outside the womb deserve the right to do so?

Our devotion to our cause should not determine what is right. It must be devotion to the truth. The truth is that babies are being terminated within the womb who could live outside the womb if given the opportunity. Who will speak for them? One of the subtle tricks of the serpent has once again been woven into the minds of intelligent women and men. It is often seen that the very thing that gave birth to a movement is rejected by the same movement in future generations. The extremist feminist movement, by virtue of Roe vs. Wade, apparently failed to realize that they have effectively eliminated the power of millions of women's voices that will never be. In their fury to demand rights over their own bodies, they have suffocated into silence the voices of multitudes of their future daughters and sisters. How many of these would have grown up to be brilliant, articulate, and powerful women who would have positively influenced their culture? The absence of their voices is an indictment upon us all.

As I wrote in chapter fourteen, there is always a battle over the seed a woman carries. I believe that the conscience of America is being awakened, and America will use her powerful voice to repent and change this deadly mindset.

The beauty of a democratic society is that true freedom allows individuals to use that freedom according to their own conscience within certain parameters prescribed by law. When one person's abuse of their freedom impinges upon or actually removes the freedoms of another— problems arise. This is where governmental legislation comes in to insure that those who abuse the system are punished and stopped. However, when legislation itself enables people to abuse the freedoms of others, the system itself becomes based on injustice. This should and does raise the ire of both God and man. As C. S. Lewis said, *"Education without values, as useful as it is, seems rather to make man a more clever devil."*

When a man is placed in fetters and forced to work for nothing because his skin is black, this is injustice. When a woman is denied the privilege of the right to cast a vote expressing the convictions of her conscience because of her gender, this is injustice. When an unborn child is denied the

> **The fact that a person is born male or female does not determine the value of the personage.**

right to experience the life that he/she already possesses, this is injustice. The color of one's skin is not a determination of human worth. The fact that a person is born male or female does not determine the value of the personage. The fact that a human being is still in the womb of his/her mother does not diminish the value of their human dignity. Ethnicity, sex, or age should not remove the responsibility of the state to legislate parameters to protect the freedoms of all its people .

In the beginning, humans were not intended to be the slaves of other human beings. In the beginning, Adam and Eve were both given dominion to rule and reign in partnership together. Removing the yoke of slavery from human beings moved civilization closer to Eden. Restoring the power of a woman's voice is a step toward the place Eve left in Eden.

However, to use this thinking to apply to the issue of one's sexual preference is an altogether different scenario. This is where the mindset can become twisted again. To equate gay rights with civil rights or women's rights or the rights of the unborn is a misalignment of the basic foundational facts at hand.

The moment a child is born, their sex is already determined. All throughout human history birth announcements have been made with, "It's a boy!" or "It's a girl!" Fathers and mothers have joyfully shared, "I have a daughter!" or "I have a son!" All through human history in order for a child to be born, it took a man supplying the seed and the woman supplying the egg. The birth of a child is impossible without the contribution of both. When a person is born, their skin color is inherent and cannot be changed. To legislate protection for people based on a behavior is not consistent with what was in the heart of the original women's rights activists or civil rights activists. People demanding equal rights based on their sexual preference is completely different than people demanding equal rights based on their sex. One is based on what a person chooses to do; the other is based on who a person is created to be. To say, God created a person "gay" is to declare null and void what the Bible records God originally decreed.

Gen 1:27 So God created man in His own image; in the image of God He created him; male and female He created them.

God created man, and God created woman. There are two sexes in the human race, and they both were ordained and created by God. The enemy works to distort God's original intentions in an attempt to stop the restoration of all things and his own final demise. Jesus also reiterated this truth.

Mark 10:6 But from the beginning of the creation, God made them male and female .

A man who declares he was created for another man or a woman who declares she was created for another woman is out of harmony with God's original intention for them. Their thinking and desires are being fueled by the deception of the fallen world. When man's laws are in line with God's laws, then there is favor. When they collide, there is judgment.

People can behave as they wish, but they suffer the consequences that come when they violate law. The basis of law must be rooted in some standard. Our nation has been grounded on the truths contained in the Old Testament and New Testament Scriptures. As such we have a Judeo/Christian foundation as a nation. This does not mean that others cannot worship as they please. It does mean that our law rests upon divine revelation. To change the foundation is to risk the collapse of the whole structure. This is the reason the battle for a traditional understanding of marriage is so important.

> **To change the foundation is to risk the collapse of the whole structure.**

Removing protection from the unborn and redefining what marriage has always meant is contrary to the original foundations of our society and moves our society in the wrong direction. *Wrong* meaning the direction that will cause us to unravel and lose the fabric that holds society together and makes it work. I share this section so that it is clearly seen that not all women's rights issues are aimed in the right direction.

Allow me to conclude with the following summation:

What are the facts?

Fact One--Men and women are different, but we can be different and still be equal in worth. A Ford and a Chevrolet are both automobiles, but they are different. Chocolate ice cream and vanilla ice cream are both ice cream, but they are different. K-Mart and Wal-Mart are both large retail chains, but they are different. Starbucks and Joe Muggs are both coffee shops, but they are different. The Dallas Cowboys and the Washington Redskins are both football teams, but they are different and some years they are very different. I know the analogies break down at given points, but the main point is that man and woman are both human beings, but they are different. Eve was created from Adam and brought to Adam from God to bring completion to Adam and fulfillment to God's purposes for creating humankind. The truth is both man and woman need each other in order to fulfill God's purposes in the earth.

Fact Two—Only a man can father a child. The man provides the spermatozoa and the woman the egg. It takes both for conception to take place.

Fact Three—Only a woman can carry and birth a child. To use the vernacular, it takes two to tango. God's purpose of being fruitful and multiplying and filling the earth with children required both Adam and Eve. This would only happen if they were in relationship with one another. For it to happen in any other way would require a forcing of one or the other's will. This is called rape, and it is a very wrong, heinous sin and crime against humanity and God's intentions for humanity. The woman was created physiologically and psychologically to mother her children.

Fact Four—Only a woman is equipped by nature to feed a newborn child. A man does not have the ability to provide milk for a child. It is the woman whom God intended to nurse the child. Daddy can feed the child later as the child develops but when a baby is born, mother has God given means to feed her child.

Fact Five—A man and a woman become one in marriage. Procreation was ordained to happen out of a permanent commitment called marriage that a man and a woman both enter into willingly.

Fact Six—Man and woman have a natural attraction toward each other. God created man and woman to have desires for relationship with the opposite sex. As He brought Eve to Adam, He will also lead individuals today to each other.

Fact Seven—Only a woman has a monthly cycle. Each month a woman's body releases an egg into her womb that has the capacity to be fertilized by the man's sperm. When it does not conceive, it is eliminated through the menstrual cycle.

Fact Eight—Man was created first. Adam was created first, and then the woman (later named Eve) was made from his side. Man came from dust which was made by God. It was the creative power of God that made man from the dust. Adam was made by the God who made the dust.

Fact Nine—Woman was created from man. Woman was made from a rib taken out of Adam's side. The substance of her origin was man. The source of her origin was the creative power of God. She was made by the God who made the rib.

Fact Ten—Man is born from woman; and woman is impregnated by man. Man continues to exist because of the capacity of woman to carry life in her womb. She is able to carry life in the womb because of the seed that the man supplies. Both man and woman are essential to the plans and purposes of God in the earth. This is true physically and spiritually. In coming together there is a multiplication both physically and spiritually. Simply put—we need each other and should war against the forces that try to destroy either of us. The enemy desires us to separate or to completely disregard all our differences. We were made to be different, but we were made for each other. Men and women are equal but not identical.

209

Chapter Seventeen
Slowly, but Surely!

"People don't resist change. They resist being changed"! — *Peter Senge*

~

Times are slowly changing for women, and I believe the days of acceleration for the restoration of women are coming. In the Old Testament, ancient Israel was given the admonition by the Lord that when they entered the Promised Land they would take it little by little.

Deut 7:22 And the LORD your God will drive out those nations before you little by little; you will be unable to destroy them at once, lest the beasts of the field become too numerous for you. 23 But the LORD your God will deliver them over to you, and will inflict defeat upon them until they are destroyed.

The context of this verse relates how they would possess the land promised to them once they crossed the Jordan. All of the land was theirs by promise before they ever set foot upon it. Yet they had to walk it out in real-time. The Promised Land for New Testament believers is our position in Christ and all the benefits He makes available to us. However, we too, must walk it out in real time. Our sanctification (to be set apart or made holy) is realized throughout the course of our lives as we find victory in one area and then another. This little by little principle is also applicable to the kingdom. It is being expanded one person at a time, one issue at a time (Isaiah 28:10).

Throughout the history of the Church, we have seen gains and setbacks. The Deuteronomy 7 passage just referred to tells us that all the territory was not to be taken at once because the beasts of the field would become too numerous. There is a sense is which more ground can be gained than can be cared for. The biblical model seems to be—take some ground, fortify it, settle it, and then take more ground. *Too much, too soon*, has been the downfall of many believers and congregations. *Slowly, but surely,* sees steady progress. In the realm of the spirit, I imagine that where the enemy sees great advances being made, he sends his demonic troops by the hordes to stop it. In the advance of the kingdom, the days do arrive when we see the Jordan parted, Jericho's walls fall, and great breakthrough happening. The women's issue will be no different. Following is a story of another one of my little by little breakthrough moments:

In June of 2000, I was invited to be one of the speakers at a pastors' conference in Florence, Alabama, where pastors from around the country came together for a time of refreshing. The other speakers for the conference where Johnny Wade and Diane Sloan, a husband and wife team who were from Hamilton, Ohio. Johnny Wade was the main speaker for the evening services, and Diane and I were to share each morning. The conference started on a Monday night, so the first opportunity I had to minister was on Tuesday morning. Diane spoke first that morning, and I followed her. As I made my way to the podium, something started happening to me. I felt the conviction of the Holy Spirit, and I became aware the Lord was requiring me to deal with something else before I could preach. I remembered the many times I had spoken against God speaking through a woman. I remembered the conversations I had engaged in with my buddies in which we refuted the notion of God speaking through women. I realized at that moment a very wrong heart issue behind my conversations. It was as if the woman issue was not the issue at all at that

> **Conviction came upon me convincing me that I was wrong in how I had responded to women in ministry.**

moment. The issue was the matter of my heart. At that moment, I realized it was not about "What the Bible Said"; it was about what I had thought and said. Conviction came upon me convincing me that I was wrong in how I had responded to women in ministry. It's hard to explain, but I knew that I could not preach until I got my heart right. I stood behind the pulpit for a few moments composing myself and gathering my thoughts. I then shared with the audience that there was something I needed to do before I

213

ministered to them. I proceeded to ask Diane to forgive me for all the words I had spoken against women in ministry throughout my years as a pastor. I acknowledged the pride in my heart in thinking I was superior to women in the kingdom, and I confessed the sin of refusing to receive ministry from women. I affirmed that it was obvious that God's hand was upon Diane and that I had been wrong about the women in ministry issue. After I did this, I felt the burden released and knew I had experienced another mini-breakthrough in my thinking. Afterwards, Diane graciously expressed her gratitude to my obedience. Incidentally, I now pastor the congregation where that conference was held.

It is also interesting that years ago, the church I now pastor had a woman, Clara Peterson, as its pastor for a couple of years. The Pastor Emeritus, as I lovingly refer to as Granddaddy Pastor, is Henry Melton He pastored the church for forty-two years before placing the baton in my hand. He shared with me that Pastor Clara taught his wife how to cook drop biscuits in the basement of the church. This little snapshot of life in the 1940's demonstrates that Pastor Clara Peterson did not feel that being a pastor conflicted with her being a woman who enjoyed cooking. In a way Faith Church, (formerly Faith Tabernacle Church), was a forerunner in the area of the restoration of the voice of women in our area. There was a time in my ministerial life that I would have never dreamed of considering pastoring a church that had previously had a woman as a pastor.

About three years ago, my wife and I were at a small meeting with a few other ministers from the mid-South region of the country. James Goll was presiding at the meeting. James is a precious prophetic brother from Franklin, Tennessee, who is widely sought as a conference speaker. He also is a prolific author. At the meeting, he prophesied over Mikki and me as well as our congregation. We have the prophetic word recorded, and recently Mikki and I pulled it out and prayed over it. As we did, we were amazed at how the word connected to what God was doing in the writing of this book as well. Part of what James spoke concerning our congregation touched the issue of women:

"The Lord is going to do something real distinct also in your house. You know because I have been there, and I know your house. He is going to use women in your house. And there is going to be particular women from the outside who come into this house. And the women are going to carry a key of the breaker anointing. And so receive the servants and servantists of the Lord. They will come if you send the call. They will come, and there will be a breaker anointing that will come specifically on women. There will be Deborahs raised up in this house—Deborahs! It is like a school of Deborahs shall come forth in this house. But Deborah had Barak. And Deborahs function where there is security. And the Lord is going to use you as a couple to model something

together…..Now that this place of security in identity in the breaker anointing shall be released in this house and there will be incredible celebrations of praise, and the warrior mantle and the bridal garment will be woven together,…. "

In April of 2007, Kingdom Alignment Ministries led by Tammy Alsup, is holding a conference at Faith Church. Tammy is a woman whom God is using strategically on a national level to network congregations, ministries, and ministers together to advance the kingdom. At the conference will be Jane Hansen, Peter Wagner, and Barbara Yoder, as well as others. Barbara Yoder wrote the book, *The Breaker Anointing*. This was not put together to fulfill a word; it came together by the Spirit and the Lord has reminded us of the Word given three years ago. It is truly awesome how God weaves our destinies together to fulfill His purposes in the earth. I am excited about what will happen.

This past year we made several changes pertaining to our congregation we felt needed to be made. We changed the name of the church from Faith Tabernacle to Faith Church. Sometimes it is important to change names to reflect the now thing God is doing. We chose to simply call the church Faith Church because we are composed of people from every denominational stripe you can think of. I humorously tell our people that we should be called the—

Pente-Metho-Bapticostal-Independent-Charismatic-Presbypalian-Church-of-Christ!

Getting this on the sign by the road would be problematic, so we just chose Faith Church. Another area of change that relates to the writing of this book was a change in the Constitution and By-laws of the church. In order to be a legally incorporated entity, a church has to have a written document that expresses the guidelines and purposes of its existence. Our Constitution forbade women from having a voice in the decisions of the church. The church no longer aligned with this so we decided to change it. Once we changed this in the natural, I began receiving revelation in the Spirit concerning the voice of women in God's kingdom. I know the church I pastor is just a microcosm of what God is doing globally to bring together the restoration of the voice of women.

Interestingly, the first woman in our county of the state to ever be elected into the higher level of state government, was just elected to serve as State Representative of District 1. Her name is Tammy Irons. Also, the first woman to ever serve as Chief Justice of the Alabama Supreme Court was just sworn into office. On a national level, the first woman to ever do so, has just been elected to sit as Speaker of the House of Representatives. These are all changes that reflect the rise of the voice of women to a new level in our culture. Often, the natural reflects what is going on in the spiritual as well. More and more women are taking their places in the government of the kingdom in the earth. Again, realize this is not about women abdicating the distinct roles they have been given because they are women; it is about being allowed to assume all the roles that God has given them in the kingdom. It is not about taking the man's place; it is about her taking her place along side the man. It was Thomas Jefferson who said, *"Every generation needs a new revolution."* These are days of revolutionary changes in the body of Christ. Things are slowly but surely changing as women take their place at the side of men in God's glorious kingdom.

Chapter Eighteen
What's a Woman Worth?

The day will come when men will recognize woman as his peer, not only at the fireside, but in councils of the nation. Then, and not until then, will there be the perfect comradeship, the ideal union between the sexes that shall result in the highest development of the race. —Susan B. Anthony

~

- Were women created just to have babies?
- Was God's intention for a woman purely biological?
- Is the worth of a woman always in regard to her relationship with a man?
- Why is she here?
- What is her role in God's plan of the ages?
- Is her goal limited to cooking, cleaning, and keeping the man's bed warm?
- Is she to be allowed to release her voice in power and authority in the kingdom?
- As important as it may be, is she limited to sharing her heart with only children?

These are just questions! But how you answer these questions is very important. What God says is even more important.

I believe God's original intention for women is far above what culture has been able to perceive. Her place in God's unfolding of history is much more important that most men and women have allowed. Through the annals of time, men's opinions about the worth of women have been rather low.

> **Is the Word diminished when it is gazed upon and studied by women? Does it lose its power if it is spoken out of the mouth of a woman?**

Eliezer, a Jewish Rabbi of the first century, wrote, *"Rather should the words of the Torah be burned than entrusted to a woman."* Scholars today mix words over what Rabbi Eliezer meant but it seems clear that he felt a woman and the study of the Torah should not go together. He went on to say, *"Whoever teaches his daughter the Torah is like one who teaches her obscenity."* [40] Again it seems clear that he saw the role of women as being disconnected from being taught the first five books of the Old Testament. To me it appears that this teacher of the Torah saw woman's status as being too low to handle God's Holy Word. Are women to study God's Word? Is the Word diminished when it is gazed upon and studied by women? Does it lose its power if it is spoken out of the mouth of a woman? Are the promises less sure when delivered by women?

Bruce Metzger, a well-respected scholar of biblical studies, informs us of the status of women during biblical times: "They had become second-class Jews, excluded from the worship and teaching of God, with status scarcely above that of slaves."[41] This demonstrates how radical it was for Jesus to minister to women in the way that He did. Jesus was the greatest teacher who has ever taught God's Word, and His audience included women. Since He directly taught them God's Word, it seems safe to assume that He saw them as learners (disciples) in His classroom. He taught women while they were with men and upon occasion He taught a woman one on one—the Samaritan woman at the well. When He taught all day and then miraculously fed over five thousand people with a few fish and loaves--men, women, and children were present.[42]

Tertullian, one of the early church fathers, gives us insight into how many men of his day viewed women:

> Do you not know that you are each an Eve? The sentence of God on this sex of yours lives in this age: the guilt must of necessity live, too. You are the Devil's gateway: You are the unsealer of the forbidden tree: You are the first deserter of the divine law: You are she who persuaded him whom the devil was not valiant enough to attack. You destroyed so easily God's image, man. On account of your desert even the Son of God had to die. *St. Tertullian (155 to 225 A.D.):*[43]

Notice the conclusions that can be drawn from what Tertullian had to say about women in this quote.

- Every woman still bears the guilt of Eve.
- God's judgment on women has not been removed.
- The devil still targets women as his gateway to humanity.
- Woman destroyed man who was God's image.
- Woman was weaker and inferior to man even before sin entered the human race.
- Woman alone bears the blame for Jesus having to die.

A couple of centuries later, the attitude toward women among theologians hadn't seemed to change much as indicated by the comments of Augustine. *"What is the difference whether it is in a wife or a mother, it is still Eve the temptress that we must beware of in any woman."* Augustine further stated, *"I fail to see what use woman can be to man, if one excludes the function of bearing children."* St. Augustine of Hippo (354 to 430 A.D.). It is true that some women have seduced men into sin. It is also true that some men have seduced women into sin. The fact is that Eve was herself deceived by the serpent. To make her the "Satan" of the world is far fetched.

I quoted from Augustine earlier in the book in regard to his theology of sin. This shows us that the same man can be very right in some areas and very wrong in others. Men should not be followed blindly but should be held to the standard of Scripture. These early views on women show us

222

that the worth of women in many men's minds was relegated to the act of procreation. The idea of a woman being powerfully used of God in the area of ministry doesn't seem to coincide with the thinking of men in the early centuries.

> The idea of a woman being powerfully used of God in the area of ministry doesn't seem to coincide with the thinking of men in the early centuries.

Even in the era of the Protestant Reformation, Martin Luther taught that woman's primary use was to bear children. "Even though they grow weary and wear themselves out with child-bearing, it does not matter; let them go on bearing children till they die, that is what they are there for."[44] Certainly women are the bearers of children, but is that all? Can you imagine how women down through the centuries who were hungry for God felt as they watched the men go inside to be taught God's Word while they remained on the outside looking in? Is the Old Testament separation that kept women in the outer court still valid for today? Did Jesus tear down the wall or not?

Today the issue of women being educated and allowed to study still exists. And it is not just the Bible they are not allowed to be taught. Many women around the world do not have the opportunity to learn. On September 18, 2006, in the New York City Public Library, First Lady Laura Bush addressed the audience gathered at the White House

Conference on Global Literacy. She stated, "Across the globe, more than 800 million people are illiterate. One hundred million children are not in school, which means they're not learning to read. And of the 771 million adults who cannot read a simple book, more than two-thirds of them are women."[45] This means that more than 514 million adult women around the world cannot read. It also means that there are two illiterate women for every illiterate man. Women today are still being deprived of the opportunity of education.

Is the value of a woman to be reduced to purely biological terms? Is it her body and its capacities to bear children alone that is of value? Surely there is intrinsic worth carried by a woman. God's Word declares that she is made in the image of God as man is. The first man recognized the first woman as being like himself. When God presented the woman to Adam, what was his response?

Gen 2:23 And Adam said:
"This is now bone of my bones
And flesh of my flesh;
She shall be called Woman,
Because she was taken out of Man."

Adam recognized and valued the woman. He acknowledged that she was like him. He demonstrated respect for her when he said she is flesh of my flesh. In the beginning, it was clear to see that Adam saw Eve as his equal. God gave both of them dominion and authority. They were declared to be one.

Charles Wesley, brother of the famed, John Wesley wrote a blessed view of woman in one of his hymns which gave woman a place of privilege in a day when she was denied it by most.

Not from his head was woman took,
As made her husband to o'erlook;
Not from his feet, as one designed
The footstool of the stronger kind;
But fashioned for himself, a bride;
An equal, taken from his side.

On July 19-20, 1848, at the Wesleyan Chapel in Seneca Falls, New York, the first women's rights convention was held in the United States. There were over 300 people in attendance, and a document was signed called the Declaration of Sentiments. It laid out the injustices that women faced in being denied rights that men were freely afforded. In those days, "women were not allowed the freedoms assigned to men in the eyes of the law, the church, or the government. Women did not vote, hold elected office, attend college, or earn a living. If married, they could not make legal contracts, divorce an abusive husband, or gain custody of their children."[46] This meeting became the beginning of a movement that would finally see women given the right to vote. The Declaration of Sentiments was written to reflect the sound and style of the Declaration of Independence. It is included in aApendix II in the back of this book for those who may enjoy reading it.

Progress has been made in restoring the respect and value of women, but the task that lies ahead is still formidable. It is the truths contained in the liberating Gospel of Jesus Christ that will change the mindsets of people and bring down the strongholds embedded in a culture. These strongholds are easily detected. Globally, it is the women who are in areas where the Gospel has not penetrated that are repressed the greatest.

Today in many countries women are not provided the healthcare needed and the practice of child brides is still costing the lives of little girls who become pregnant before their bodies can physiologically handle birth. According to the U. S. State Department in their 2006 Fall Edition of the International Women's Issues Newsletter, "Worldwide approximately 529,000 women die each year from maternal causes, and for every woman that dies, 20 more suffer injuries, infection and disabilities in pregnancy or childbirth. In child marriages, factors such as underdeveloped physiology and lack of information and access to services heighten these risks. In many instances maternal deaths are the result of lack of access to health care in developing countries."[47]

Globally, women are still not fully recognized for their contribution to the workforce and for their role in providing for their families. Richard H. Robbins made the following observation:

At the same time that women produce 75 to 90 percent of food crops in the world, they are responsible for the running of households. According to the United Nations, in no country in the world do men come anywhere close to women in the amount of time spent in housework. Furthermore, despite the efforts of feminist movements, women in the core [wealthiest, Western countries] still suffer disproportionately, leading to what sociologists refer to as the "feminization of poverty," where two out of every three poor adults are women. The informal slogan of the Decade of Women became "Women do two-thirds of the world's work, receive 10 percent of the world's income and own 1 percent of the means of production."[48]

Honor killings in Pakistan for trivial reasons, genital mutilation of women by Islamic fundamentalists that steal from young girls the possibility of ever enjoying a sexual experience with their future husbands, trafficking young women out of Ukraine for sexual predators, the global problem of rape and incest, unfair lending practices of banks that discriminate against women, and religiously driven wife beating and abuse are just some of the problems that women are having to contend with in today's modern world. The world is more modern, but the same old ancient curse is still at work. God has something better in store for these descendents of Eve.

Chapter Nineteen
Ending the Domination of Women

Something which we think is impossible now is not impossible in another decade. — Constance Baker Motley, First African American Woman in the U.S. to become a Federal Judge

~

Man was created first and then woman—this is clear. But does "first" imply "foremost"? Paul taught that God was the head of Christ, but that does not mean that God was superior to Christ. The Bible teaches the full deity of Jesus Christ as God. So then, headship has more to do with a function than with superiority. Man and woman were created as equals, but the man was created first. Throughout the Bible man has been given the role of headship in marriage. Paul clearly sets this forth in his letter to the Ephesians.[49] The man should be the spiritual leader in the marriage. Marriage is a microcosm of the church. As Christ watches over His bride—the church—to love, nurture, and protect her, so should every husband do so to his wife. This is when they together are most fulfilled.

However, he is not to use the call he has for his own marriage as a justification to submit all women to himself. I should not attempt to be head of someone else's wife. No man would want his wife to submit to another man as she would to him. The submission in marriage is about intimacy and being in oneness so the fruitfulness of God's plans and

> ...headship has more to do with a function than with superiority.

purposes can be experienced in our lives. This does not mean a wife shouldn't be involved in decision making in the marriage. Man's role in marriage as the head is in order for true oneness to be experienced in the marriage. In order for believers to really enjoy oneness with Christ, we have to submit to Him.

When we gather as a church, we are all the bride positionally and relationally to Christ. Just as the church submits to Christ's love and desires to carry out His purposes in the earth, so should a wife submit to her husband and the God given desires and purposes he carries in His heart. When the husband is submitting to the Lord and the wife is submitting to the Lord and her husband, then everything is in order. When he or she steps out of submission to Christ, the oneness and intentions of God are not realized in the marriage. Paul further states that we are to also submit to one another. In other words, it is to be the giving of our hearts to one another in service and love. There is no hint of domination. When an attitude of domination enters into leadership at any level, a tyrant has arrived.

All this means that the wife stands at the side of her husband and brings her wisdom and resources into the marriage in order for both of them to complete what God wants. This was the order of Eden. Remember, the woman is the helper, the one who provides what the man does not have in order for God's purposes to be completed.

It is true that women live in a world dominated by men. This, however, was not the way it was originally intended to be. There is a vast difference between headship and dominance. Dominion was part of God's original plan for both men and women. This is clear from the biblical record.

Gen 1:27 So God created man in His own image; in the image of God He created him; male and female He created them. 28 Then God blessed them, and God said to them, "Be fruitful and multiply; fill the earth and subdue it; have dominion over the fish of the sea, over the birds of the air, and over every living thing that moves on the earth."

Notice that the text reads, *and God said to THEM...(Emphasis added)*

Dominion was given to both of them—the man and the woman together. Notice also that there is no mention of exercising dominion over each other or over other human beings. War, slavery, sadomasochism, child abuse, sexual abuse and many other problems are the direct result of one or more human beings dominating someone else. Domination creates a relationship based on an unhealthy fear.

God specified the sphere of dominion that men and women were freely given to express and enjoy. The dominion was over the sphere of Earth and all other forms of life on the earth. Isn't it also interesting that it was through the serpent that Satan deceived the woman and led the man into sin? Theologically, sin came because the first couple disobeyed the clear command of God not to eat of the tree of the knowledge of good and evil. In listening to the serpent, Eve submitted where she had been given dominion. God clearly said that they were to exercise dominion over "every living thing that moves upon the earth."(Gen. 1:28) This included the serpent. In submitting to the serpent, rebellion was committed against God. Why were Adam and Eve given this dominion in the realm of the earth? If they had not been given authority over all the created order, they could not have been exclusively submitted to God. The only authority humanity had to answer to was God. This is the way it will be once again whenever thing is restored and Satan, the usurper, is eternally dealt with.

David caught a glimpse of our lofty privilege and was in awe of our place in the created order when he exclaimed:

Ps 8:3 When I consider Your heavens, the work of Your fingers,
The moon and the stars, which You have ordained,
4 What is man that You are mindful of him,
And the son of man that You visit him?
5 For You have made him a little lower than the angels,
And You have crowned him with glory and honor.

6 You have made him to have dominion over the works of Your hands;
You have put all things under his feet,
7 All sheep and oxen —
Even the beasts of the field,
8 The birds of the air,
And the fish of the sea
That pass through the paths of the seas.
9 O LORD, our Lord,
How excellent is Your name in all the earth!

The word translated "angels" in verse five is the Hebrew word "Elohim" which means God. It is the same word found in the early chapters of Genesis in reference to God Himself. David understood that God, the Creator of all that there is, created man just beneath Himself and entrusted to man authority over everything else He had created. Of course there are angels, but they are not superior to us. The angels created by God will be subject to us in judgment one day. Paul stated in the New Testament that we will judge the angels.[50] When you think of man's dominion in these terms, you realize the potential that humanity has when they cease warring between themselves and seek the highest good for the earth according to God's intentions. In order to do this, one has to decide what will be the ultimate source of truth and revelation for their life.

> **It is not what a person believes about something that makes that something what it is.**

A laissez-faire approach to truth that sees all religions as expression of the same truth is unacceptable. When one man tells a lie, someone else calling his lie the truth only creates another lie. Believing sulfuric acid is water will not keep it from killing you when you drink it. It is seeing sulfuric acid for what it really is that will protect you from drinking it. You could conceivably know that it is sulfuric acid, but if you believed sulfuric acid would not harm you, it still would eat your insides away when you drank it. It is not what a person believes about something that makes that something what it is. It only communicates what you believe about that something. Believing a dog is a cat does not make it one. It simply reveals that you do not really know what a dog is or what a cat is. Beauty is within the eyes of the beholder, but truth rests ultimately in One Source. This does not mean that anything or everything else is untrue. It simply means that ultimately there is one point, one place, one person, one source from which truth

234

originated. Who you believe to be that source reveals whom you worship or what you worship.

C.S. Lewis, who possessed one of the most brilliant and articulate minds in recent generations, said:

> These, then, are the two points I wanted to make. First, that human beings, all over the earth, have this curious idea that they ought to behave in a certain way, and cannot really get rid of it. Secondly, that they do not in fact behave in that way. They know the Law of Nature; they break it. These two facts are the foundation of all clear thinking about ourselves and the universe we live in.[51]

This Law of Nature that Lewis refers to reveals that men and women around the planet feel that they are accountable to someone or something out there for how they live their lives. This someone or something also causes us to sense accountability to our fellow human beings as well. Someone who exhibits no sense of accountability to others will soon be labeled a criminal, a madman, or a monster. Such was the case of Adolf Hitler who saw no value in a Jew, a minority, the handicapped, or mentally challenged. So he engineered their elimination (murder). He is now viewed to be what he really was, though for a season, because a mass of people were deceived, he was seen to be someone totally different than who he, in fact, really was.

So then we see that what we believe is important. But more importantly, we must believe what is true. How could people of Hitler's day have concluded sooner who he really was? By having a standard of truth—of what is truly right or wrong- particularly when it comes to the "big" issues— the value of human life. Our source of truth has to be rooted in what God has said, not in the cultural mindsets of the people regardless of the age in which they might live.

When it comes to truth, each person puts their own eggs in one basket. What you believe to be the source of truth forms the foundation of all your mindsets, decisions, and life in general.

God's original intention was for man and woman to reflect His image and be bearers of His glory in the earth. They were to fill it with sons and daughters who would do the same. He, Father God, would relate to them as His children. By the way, when it is all said and done, He will see this desire fulfilled in the age to come. His children, those redeemed in Christ, will exercise His authority in the realm of Earth to His honor and glory. We have been adopted into His family by the blood of Jesus through His Holy Spirit. As the Church, we are advancing His kingdom in the realm of Earth. This time we do it with the full knowledge that Satan is opposed to us and trying to deceive us. I encourage you to read the challenge issued by a study group affiliated with the Lausanne Conference that is composed of Christian leaders from around the world. You will find the *Issue Group 24 Statement* in Appendix I at the back of the book. It sets forth the mindsets needed in the body of Christ to see the restoration of women. When we look at God's original intentions with the understanding that Father really does know best, we see the wonder of paradise. We also begin to see some of the steps we need to take to unwind the suffocating coils of the serpent's suppression off the lives of men and women.

Domination of one person over another regardless of gender is a result of sin. We have taken great steps in eliminating the slavery issue where humans serve as "Masters" over other humans, but we have work to do to see the restoration of the mindset of men ruling over women. Authority and dominion go hand in hand. Domination, however, implies a forced subjugation. Even God, the ultimate authority, did not force Adam and Eve to serve Him. The basis of slavery itself is the idea of forced subjugation.

When Adam and Eve chose to submit to someone other than God, He exercised His authority and expelled them from the garden. But His expulsion of the first couple from the Garden of Eden was not done in a mean and hasty fashion, it was done redemptively. Once out of the Garden, they were free to choose once again the path God had chosen for them. Their choices would be through struggle and war due to the curse of sin upon the earth and the seed of sin that had rooted in their hearts. Their nature had become corrupted through their personal experience with sin. They certainly passed the story of their former glory and sinful failure on to their offspring. Abel, their second-born son, is seen offering an acceptable sacrifice to the Lord with a heart that desired to be right. Cain, their first-born son, repeated the sin of his parents in an increased capacity—he became angry at God and his brother. With a heart filled with anger, hate, and jealousy, he killed his brother and then tried to deny what he had done. The root of sin and deception was seen vividly in Cain. The longing to see things restored was seen in Abel. It seems the serpent struck the first family again and used the first seed out of the woman's womb to kill the second seed out of the woman's womb.

Adam and Eve then watched their first-born son leave their presence as he was banished to a place removed from them. They must have felt a little of what God felt as He witnessed them leaving Eden because of their sin. The image of their Father in them had been severely damaged, but I believe that even lost humanity today still bears the image of God in the earth. This image is not what it was in the beginning by a long shot, but it has not been completely obliterated as some would have us believe. Man has no ability within himself to restore what was lost in Eden. God had to act on His behalf to see the precious relationship that was lost in

Eden restored to its intended glory. Likewise, in order for man and woman to properly relate, God has to act on their behalf. This is why the marriage ceremony is so vitally important. A man and a woman come together at an altar. The altar is simply the place where the man and the woman come together before God and humanity to enter into a covenant relationship. Someone who is invested with authority presides over the ceremony and makes a legal pronouncement that the two have become one. The marriage is seen as valid and vital by God and by humanity. It is protected by the earthly government who has been given authority by God Himself to provide peace and protection to the people within its sphere.

Human law was, in part, initiated to define how far humanity could freely express its own choices. These boundaries helped serve as a motivation to put the brakes on humanity's run-away nature. Even the Garden of Eden had boundaries. These boundaries served a similar purpose. The moment the boundary (*no eating from the tree of the knowledge of good and evil*) was broken, consequences would be incurred.

It is also interesting that before God created the woman, He healed the wound in Adam's side. I believe this is a prophetic

It is also interesting that before God created the woman, He healed the wound in Adam's side.

239

snapshot for us men. We all need to be healed of our wounds so that we can fully accept woman as God made her. It is also a beautiful truth relating to marriage. A woman who has met God is brought into the life of a man who has met God by the hand of God. A man needs to be healed of his wounds before he can properly receive the woman into his life. It is important that they are both healed from the wounds in their lives by allowing the hand of God to touch them where they have been hurt. When they are brought together in marriage, God's math kicks in--1+1=1. The Bible says that the two become one. This is the wonder and mystery of marriage. The serpent has always fought with all the demonic forces he can muster to tear up the communication and relationship between men and women. It started in Eden but it will end before the paradise to come arrives. The first place this restoration should be seen is within the body of Christ where we all enjoy the love of our bridegroom—Jesus.

To tamper with the sacred institution of marriage is within itself another strategy of the serpent to further deteriorate the relationship between men and women. Perhaps all of this is simpler than we have made it to be. The woman was made by God to be the human carrier of the next generation while it is at its most vulnerable point. A child needs his/her Mother's care and nurture. Eve possessed the attributes of Adam, but she also was made so that God could continue His creativity activity through her life. He made her with a womb. The miracle of this is witnessed over 350,000 times each day around the world when a woman gives birth to her child. This is evidence of God's hand continuing to work within the womb of a woman. Her existence began while Adam slept and reached within him to get what He needed to create a woman. Now God reaches into the womb of a woman and creates another human being. He uses what is contributed by the man and the woman to perpetuate the human race. This is the miracle of childbirth, and we all are the result of it. Part of the awesome role that was given man and woman was to bear children. Every child needs a father and a mother. Each contributes from their uniqueness to help a child to grow up whole, balanced, and stable.

Yes, men and women are different in many ways, but we are also the same in many ways. Some Jewish theologians teach a creation model that the first human created by God was both male and female. One side was male and the other side was female. God then separated the two sides and made them a separate man and woman. They teach that this is what is meant by God taking from Adam's side and making a woman. This may or may not be accurate, but it makes for a great picture. One thing is for sure— both man and woman were created by God. Both were made in His image. Both were given dominion and authority. The man was created first and then the woman. Both are accountable to God to be obedient and live for Him. It takes both of them working together to populate the human family. They both are to be valued and respected. They both were originally intended to walk in the earth with power and dominion as the children of God. Partnering together, they both advance the purposes of God in the realm of Earth. And very important to the conclusion of this book, they BOTH qualify through repentance and faith to be the recipients of the restorative benefits of the death, burial, and resurrection of Jesus Christ!

I trust that each of you women who have read this book will begin to look at yourself through the truth of Eden and the lens of scripture. You should see yourself through the eyes of Jesus and receive respect in light of God's estimation of who you are. You were created in power and wonder to stand along side the man as God's under regents in the earth. You also have been declared by God Himself to wage war as a warrior against Satan and his seed. You have dominion, and you are under the dominion of God alone.

Your voice is powerful.
Your call from God is strategic.
Your prayers move heaven.
Your Savior loves and honors you.
Your Father has prophesied your victory.
Your restoration is assured.
Your time is now!
Woman—YOU are who God says you are!

Appendix I

Author comment: I thank the people of the Lausanne Conference for allowing me to use this material in this book. They offer to us a declaration that calls us to empower both men and women in ministry. May God bless you as you live out the restoration power of Jesus in all areas of your life!

~Issue Group 24 Declaration~

(This declaration is from an issue paper from the 2004 Lausanne conference in Thailand entitled *Empowering Men and Women in Ministry*)

"In order that the whole Church may take the whole gospel to the whole world, we, the issue Lausanne Issue Group 24 "Empowering Men and Women for Ministry," affirm that more labourers, both men and women, must be released to exercise their God-given gifts for ministry and leadership. More than half of the body of Christ are women who are the most undervalued and under utilized resource of the Church. At this critical time the Church urgently needs to empower the ministry of women and men in full partnership. We recognize that the Bible teaches that women and men are equally:

▪ Created in God's image and likeness and entrusted

with dominion.
- Redeemed through the death of Christ.
- Gifted for ministry by the Holy Spirit.
- Called to ministry and servant leadership.
- Held responsible for using their gifts to advance the kingdom of God.

As the Church we need to:

- Repent of anything that devalues women or men.
- Embrace the teaching and example of Jesus regarding women and the Spirit-given basis for all ministry.
- Affirm the biblical basis for the equal value of men and women in advancing the gospel.
- Pray that God will break the barriers that inhibit ministry and build bridges that enable authentic partnership.
- Model, promote and celebrate mutuality in ministry.
- Invest resources that advance gift-based rather than gender-based ministry.

Appendix II
~Declaration of Sentiments~

Drafted by Elizabeth Cady Stanton and signed by 68 women and 32 men on July 20, 1848 at the first Women's Rights Convention in Seneca Falls, New York.

When, in the course of human events, it becomes necessary for one portion of the family of man to assume among the people of the earth a position different from that which they have hitherto occupied, but one to which the laws of nature and of nature's God entitle them, a decent respect to the opinions of mankind requires that they should declare the causes that impel them to such a course.

We hold these truths to be self-evident; that all men and women are created equal; that they are endowed by their Creator with certain inalienable rights; that among these are life, liberty, and the pursuit of happiness; that to secure these rights governments are instituted, deriving their just powers from the consent of the governed. Whenever any form of government becomes destructive of these ends, it is the right of those who suffer from it to refuse allegiance to it, and to insist upon the institution of a new government, laying its foundation on such principles, and organizing its powers in such form, as to them shall seem most likely to effect their safety and happiness. Prudence, indeed, will dictate that governments long established should not be changed for light and transient causes; and, accordingly, all experience hath shown that mankind are more disposed to suffer, while evils are sufferable, than to right themselves by abolishing the forms to which they were accustomed. But when a long train of abuses and usurpations, pursuing invariably the same object, evinces a design to reduce them under absolute despotism, it is their duty to throw off such government, and to provide new guards for their future security. Such has been the patient sufferance of the women under this government, and such is now the necessity which constrains them to demand the equal station to which they are entitled.

The history of mankind is a history of repeated injuries and usurpations on the part of man toward woman, having in direct object the establishment of an absolute tyranny over her. To prove this, let facts be submitted to a candid world.

He has never permitted her to exercise her inalienable right to the elective franchise.

He has compelled her to submit to laws, in the formation of which she had no voice.

He has withheld from her rights which are given to the most ignorant and degraded men - both natives and foreigners.

Having deprived her of this first right as a citizen, the elective franchise, thereby leaving her without representation in the halls of legislation, he has oppressed her on all sides.

He has made her, if married, in the eye of the law, civilly dead.

He has taken from her all right in property, even to the wages she earns.

He has made her morally, an irresponsible being, as she can commit many crimes with impunity, provided they be done in the presence of her husband. In the covenant of marriage, she is compelled to promise obedience to her husband, he becoming, to all intents and purposes, her master - the law giving him power to deprive her of her liberty, and to administer chastisement.

He has so framed the laws of divorce, as to what shall be the proper causes of divorce, in case of separation, to whom the guardianship of the children shall be given; as to be wholly regardless of the happiness of the women - the law, in all cases, going upon a false supposition of the supremacy of man, and giving all power into his hands.

After depriving her of all rights as a married woman, if single and the owner of property, he has taxed her to support a government which recognizes her only when her property can be made profitable to it.

He has monopolized nearly all the profitable employments, and from those she is permitted to follow, she receives but a scanty remuneration.

He closes against her all the avenues to wealth and distinction, which he considers most honorable to himself. As a teacher of theology, medicine, or law, she is not known.

He has denied her the facilities for obtaining a thorough education - all colleges being closed against her.

He allows her in church, as well as State, but a subordinate position, claiming Apostolic authority for her exclusion from the ministry, and, with some exceptions, from any public participation in the affairs of the Church.

He has created a false public sentiment by giving to the world a different code of morals for men and women, by which moral delinquencies which exclude women from society, are not only tolerated but deemed of little account in man.

He has usurped the prerogative of Jehovah Himself, claiming it as his right to assign for her a sphere of action, when that belongs to her conscience and her God.

He has endeavored, in every way that he could to destroy her confidence in her own powers, to lessen her self-respect, and to make her willing to lead a dependent and abject life.

Now, in view of this entire disfranchisement of one-half the people of this country, their social and religious degradation, - in view of the unjust laws above mentioned, and because women do feel themselves aggrieved, oppressed, and fraudulently deprived of their most sacred rights, we insist that they have immediate admission to all the rights and privileges which belong to them as citizens of these United States.

In entering upon the great work before us, we anticipate no small amount of misconception, misrepresentation, and ridicule; but we shall use every instrumentality within our power to effect our object. We shall employ agents, circulate tracts, petition the State and national Legislatures, and endeavor to enlist the pulpit and the press in our behalf. We hope this Convention will be followed by a series of Conventions, embracing every part of the country.

Firmly relying upon the final triumph of the Right and the True, we do this day affix our signatures to this declaration.

Appendix III

Some Scriptures to Ponder

Acts 2:17'And it shall come to pass in the last days, says God,
That I will pour out of My Spirit on all flesh;
Your sons and your daughters shall prophesy,
Your young men shall see visions,
Your old men shall dream dreams.
18 And on My menservants and on My maidservants
I will pour out My Spirit in those days;
And they shall prophesy.

Rom 16:1 I commend to you Phoebe our sister, who is a servant of the church in Cenchrea, 2 that you may receive her in the Lord in a manner worthy of the saints, and assist her in whatever business she has need of you; for indeed she has been a helper of many and of myself also.

Acts 21: 8 On the next day we who were Paul's companions departed and came to Caesarea, and entered the house of Philip the evangelist, who was one of the seven, and stayed with him. 9 Now this man had four virgin daughters who prophesied.

Rom 16:6 Greet Mary, who labored much for us. 7 Greet Andronicus and Junia, my countrymen and my fellow prisoners, who are of note among the apostles, who also were in Christ before me.

1 Cor 16:19 The churches of Asia greet you. Aquila and Priscilla greet you heartily in the Lord, with the church that is in their house.

Phil 4:2 I implore Euodia and I implore Syntyche to be of the same mind in the Lord. 3 And I urge you also, true companion, help these women who labored with me in the gospel, with Clement also, and the rest of my fellow workers, whose names are in the Book of Life.

Gal 3:26 For you are all sons of God through faith in Christ Jesus. 27 For as many of you as were baptized into Christ have put on Christ. 28 There is neither Jew nor Greek, there is neither slave nor free, there is neither male nor female; for you are all one in Christ Jesus. 29 And if you are Christ's, then you are Abraham's seed, and heirs according to the promise.

Endnotes

[1] http://www.lausanne.org/lcwe/assets/LOP53_IG24.pdf

[2] Why Not Women? A Fresh Look at Scripture on Women in Missions, Ministry, and Leadership; YWAM Publishing, Seattle, Washington, Copyright 2000.

[3] http://www.barna.org/FlexPage.aspx?Page=BarnaUpdate&BarnaUpdateID =47

[4] Ibid

[5] http://www.basicquotations.com/index.php?aid=598

[6] (from The Biblical Illustrator Copyright (c) 2002 AGES and Biblesoft, Inc.)

[7] Mishnah Avot 1.5

[8] Stoning to Death in Iran: A Crime Against Humanity Carried Out By the Mullahs' Regime

http://www.iran-e-azad.org/stoning/women.html

[9] *The Christian and The Pharisee*, by Dr. R.T, Kendall and Rabbi David Rosen, p. 77-78

[10] For the women of Iraq, the war is just beginning By Terri Judd in Basra Published: 08 June 2006 , http://news.independent.co.uk/world/middle_east/article717570.ece

[11]

http://www.iht.com/articles/ap/2006/12/03/africa/ME_GEN_Saudi_Women_S elling_Cars.php

[12] http://www.timesnews.co.ke/06dec06/magazine/magazine2.html

[13] http://www.giga-usa.com/quotes/topics/women_t006.htm

[14] http://childmolestationprevention.org/

[15] *The Complete Word Study Dictionary: Old Testament Copyright © 2003 by AMG Publishers. All rights reserved.`*

[16] I received this email from *funnycleanjokes.com.* I also have read it on multiple other humor related sites. As with many humorous stories that float on web, it is difficult to pin down where it originated. If you know, please let me know, and I will be happy to credit the creative person who blessed us with such a funny letter.

[17] Why Not Women? A Fresh Look at Scripture on Women in Missions, Ministry, and Leadership; YWAM Publishing, Seattle, Washington, Copyright 2000.

[18] From Barnes' Notes, Acts 3:21, Electronic Database Copyright © 1997, 2003 by Biblesoft, Inc. All rights reserved.

[19] *The Forerunner Anointing: Preparing for the Restoration of All Things, 2005. May be ordered from First Breath Publications at www.firstbreathministries.com.*

[20]Source: *Yes, You Can Heather!: The Story of Heather Whitestone, Miss America 1995,* by Daphne Gray with Gregg Lewis, Zondervan Publishing House, 1995.

[21] Genesis 2:18

[22] While You Were Sleeping, 1995, Caravan Pictures, Directed by Jon Turteltaub, starring Sandra Bullock and Bill Pullman, Rated PG

[23] http://humorvault.tripod.com/senior/senior_41.html

[24]George Bernard Shaw (1856 - 1950), "Pygmalion" (1913)
http://www.quotationspage.com/subjects/men+and+women/

[25] (Breath of God, p.)

[26] National Right to Life statistics,
http://www.nrlc.org/abortion/facts/abortionstats.html

[27] http://www.johnstonsarchive.net/policy/abortion/wrjp337sd.html

[28] *Washington Irving, "The Wife,"The Sketch Book, 1819-1820.*

[29] (William Ross Wallace, "The Hand That Rocks the Cradle," c.1866)

[30] (from The Complete Word Study Dictionary: Old Testament Copyright © 2003 by AMG Publishers. All rights reserved.)

[31] http://www.quotationspage.com/search.php3?homesearch=men&page=3

[32] http://members.aol.com/hywwebsite/private/joanofarc.html

[33] http://www.pbs.org/wgbh/amex/flygirls/peopleevents/pandeAMEX07.html

[34] http://www.exploratorium.edu/baseball/mitchell.html
[35] Ibid
[36] Grover Cleveland, in the *Ladies Home Journal*, April, 1905.
[37] John Adams, in a letter to Abigail Adams, February 13, 1779
[38] http://en.wikipedia.org/wiki/Abigail_Adams

[39] http://www.catholic.net/rcc/loveboth/chapter13.html
[40] Rabbi Eliezer, "*Mishnah, Sotah 3:4*"

[41] B.M. Metzger & M.D. Coogan, "*The Oxford Companion to the Bible*", Oxford University Press, New York, NY, (1993), pages 806ff

[42] Matthew 14:21
[43] http://www.piney.com/FathEnochTertu.html#P265_52058
Volume IV, Chapter One on Women and Fallen Angels

[44] http://www.giga-usa.com/quotes/authors/martin_luther_a001.htm
[45] http://www.state.gov/r/pa/ei/wh/72382.htm
[46] http://www.nps.gov/archive/wori/senecafalls1848.htm
[47] http://www.state.gov/g/wi/74751.htm#firstlady
Richard H. Robbins, Global Problems and the Culture of Capitalism, (Allyn and Bacon, 1999), p. 354
[48]
http://www.globalissues.org/HumanRights/WomensRights.asp#LackofProgress
[49] Ephesians 5:22-32
[50] 1 Corinthians 6:3

[51] Mere Christianity, by C.S. Lewis, p.7

Author Contact Information

For more information about the author and resources visit:

www.firstbreathministries.com

To schedule Eddie for a speaking engagement, call 256-767-4124.

Email can be sent to:
eddie@firstbreathministries.com

Regular Mail can be sent to:

First Breath Publications
P.O. Box 1228
Killen, Alabama 35645

Other Books Authored by Eddie Lawrence

The Forerunner Anointing
Dealing With Demons While Dancing With God
Breath of God (Nelson Books)
Marriage Roadblocks
Awaking Your Patriotic Heart

These books and other resources available at:
www.firstbreathpublications.com